What If Everything We Knew About Investing Was Wrong?

What If Everything We Knew About Investing Was Wrong?

Jeffry Haber

NorthAmerican
Business Press

Atlanta – Seattle – South Florida – Toronto

North American Business Press, Inc
Atlanta, Georgia
Seattle, Washington
South Florida
Toronto, Canada

What If Everything We Knew About Investing Was Wrong?

ISBN: 9780985394943

Along with trade books for various business disciplines, the North American Business Press also publishes a variety of academic-peer reviewed journals.

Library of Congress Control Number: 2012954584

Library of Congress
Cataloging in Publication Division
101 Independence Ave., SE
Washington, DC 20540-4320
Printed in theUnited States of America

First Edition

For Sophie,
Lauren, Amy and Jonathan

Table of Contents

List of Figures

Acknowledgements

I would first like to thank my family for supporting me in all my endeavors. Of course my wife, Holly, gets a big thank you. Before I speak at conferences Holly always reminds me that she knows about as much as I do on the subject. She keeps me grounded; very, very grounded. I also want to thank my children, Jonathan, Amy, Lauren and Sophie, who are always behind me. I am very proud of them.

I want to thank all my colleagues, some of who I count as friends, for the insights, animated conversations, and for the willingness to argue against some of my ideas. Our discussions have allowed me to develop my thinking and make this a better book. I list some, certainly not all, of my valuable colleagues. Appearing in this list should not imply agreement with anything I suggest. First, I would like to thank John Craig, Jr. for being a mentor and probably the person I have most spoken to about investing. Second is Andrew Braunstein, a trusted colleague from Iona College and my frequent co-author. Andy is a perfect complement to me and I value his thoughts and our writing relationship. I would also like to thank Gerald Chen-Young, Rich Dahab, Bruce Fetzer, Nick Gabriel, Michael Graves, Tie Kim, Mihir Meswani, Rachel Minard, Christopher Nygaard, Bob Rosenberg, and Caitlin Schryver, and I value our discussions and intellectual discourse.

From the group at Institutional Investor I would like to thank Rich Blake, Ann Cornish, Michael Ocrant, Steve Olson, Harvey Shapiro, Katarina Storfer and Lisa Yao. They produce terrific conferences and I have benefited greatly from being involved with them.

From Newton Capital Management (where I am an advisory board member) I would like to thank Jon Ritz, Jin Hill, Matt Duncan and the very talented investing team who love a good debate and have a great grasp about what they do and why they are successful.

I would also like to thank my publisher, North American Business Press, for making the publication of this book straightforward and easy.

And, of course, thank you to the reader for considering this book worthy of your time. I hope you find it interesting.

INTRODUCTION

These have been tumultuous times for those involved in investing. Since the financial crisis began in earnest in the fall of 2007 nothing has been easy in the financial markets. During this period some have wondered if we have entered a new paradigm in investing, they have examined whether old assumptions are still valid and contemplated whether previous metrics still have a place in today's investing arena. Despite the sense that the times have changed, many still cling to old methods and old ways of thinking about things. This book takes the opposite view – it wonders if everything we thought we knew about investing was wrong. It takes the most common and widely held beliefs and presents an opposing viewpoint.

Too many times I have seen people agree on points where they have no basis, no data, nothing to support their position except that "everyone knows that's the way it is." At more than one conference I have challenged these notions, asking for support for their belief. Seldom is there anything to back up their statements. Hopefully these people come away with the realization that they should do a little research (or at least a little thinking) before jumping on the bandwagon to agree with anything that builds momentum and consensus. This is not to say that they were wrong, they might very well have been correct. But they would have been correct by chance, not because they independently arrived at a similar conclusion based on data, theory or preponderance of evidence.

Looking at the financial crisis with the clarity of hindsight, investment professionals have been talking about how the "market went to 1," meaning that all asset classes became correlated as the market headed down. The implication is that there were no investment options that were going up, so the devastation to portfolios was not the fault of managers, consultants or fiduciaries, it was simply the times. Essentially, when we say the "market went to 1" we mean that there should be no accountability for those in charge of managing portfolios.

I wonder why we never say the "market went to 1" when we are riding historic bull markets on the way up. We seem to want to take credit for the good, for the consistent and significant gains, when perhaps there are few investment choices that are decreasing. In some market cycles it can be hard to pick a losing investment. But we choose not to ascribe the increase in the portfolio to the market, but instead to our investing acumen, our expertise, and our ability to ferret out well-performing investments. It is only when the market turns sour that we seek to distance ourselves from the responsibility and accountability of our actions.

To be sure, there are those that take a hard look at themselves, their decisions, and their processes. They truly yearn to be better, to learn from their mistakes, to reshape how they view the world and their portfolios' place in it. But for those that took comfort that the "market went to 1" and felt exonerated and relieved from accountability, this book has some things you may not like. The market did not go to 1. For those that say it did without nothing more than a feeling that times are bad, should get ready to be challenged, about that and a host of other widely held misconceptions.

In investing, as well as other fields, there is a tendency to hold to a party line, even in the face of information to the contrary. I wrote a paper about correlation with the idea being explored that we should consider (and I stress "consider") using streams of prices (net asset values) instead of the generally accepted use of returns. I developed various models to illustrate situations where I felt using returns in the calculation was clearly inferior. I could have accepted that the reviewer of the paper was not swayed by what I presented or found fault with my theory or found inaccuracies in my approach. But I could not accept what the reviewer wrote. Below is a part of their review:

> "The author creates numerous silly examples to contrast calculating the correlations between time series of prices and time series of returns. No one who understands the correlation statitic [sic] and the nature of price series would ever do this exercise in the first place because they would know that price series are nonstationary by construction."

The reviewer did not look at my argument. I did something that did not deserve consideration because the consensus agrees. Thankfully this reviewer did not have a say in whether Columbus' voyage should be financed since "everyone knows the earth is flat." There are many things everyone knows, right up until they find out that they were wrong. You will have an opportunity to decide for yourself whether using prices in correlation calculations should be considered.

I don't contend that anything I have written is beyond debate, to be sure there is no proof that any concept I challenge is wrong, nor that any idea I put forth is correct. Hopefully I present enough data, logic or theory so that you will agree that what I write deserves careful thought. As any academic should, I am ready to discuss and defend my positions with the understanding that I have no monopoly on truth. I could very well be wrong.

Organization

This book is organized by subject. While I do disagree with many commonly held beliefs, I try not to be disagreeable. Depending on how entrenched you are in your counter-opinions, you may not see it that way. Be that as it may, implicit on every page is an acknowledgement that I might be wrong. There is no fact in this book; it's about how we think about things and how we support our positions. I do not have a corner on truth, but then neither does anyone else.

In writing this book I have tried to bridge the gap between lay person, academic and the sophisticated investor, manager and consultant. In so doing, some explanations will seem unnecessary to many readers. I have endeavored to make the material accessible to everyone on all levels.

Chapters often start with an introduction to the subject, partly to set the stage and partly in case the reader is not familiar with the concept. The "What We Know" will be presented in bold type so that it will be hard to miss. Then I present the theory, logic and sometimes data, to hopefully frame an argument of why what we know might be wrong.

With that, let's jump right in.

-1-
<u>CORRELATION</u>

It has long been said that a diversified portfolio is the cornerstone of long-term investment performance[1]. Diversification is the concept of spreading risk through the holding of a variety of different investments. It is not hard to imagine that if our portfolio was comprised of the stock held in a single company, the portfolio will increase or decrease in direct proportion to the change in the price of that one stock. If we chose wisely, our portfolio will do very well, if not, then it will do very poorly. We would have put all our eggs in one basket. The fate of our portfolio (and perhaps the fate of our career), rests with how that one stock does.

So perhaps we would feel better about having two different stocks in our portfolio. If one does poorly, then we have the other stock to help buoy the return. Of course, we might also think that holding the stock that went down dampened the performance of the portfolio. Diversification is not about optimization. It is about providing the best opportunity for the portfolio to perform well, given the understanding that we lack reliable information about how the investments will do in the future.

Which two stocks should we pick? Whatever the first stock we add to the portfolio, we would want the second stock to be something that behaves differently in similar market conditions (if they behaved exactly the same we might as well as just doubled the quantity of the first stock and be done with it).

---

[1]There are many references I could give to support this, including the suggestion of just doing an internet search. I will select one, which comes from the Securities and Exchange Commission publication "Beginners' Guide to Asset Allocation, Diversification, and Rebalancing," available at
http://www.sec.gov/investor/pubs/assetallocation.htm.

On a small scale (such as where the shares of two companies comprise the entire portfolio), this seems like a bad idea since one stock will seem to counteract the other (if they do behave differently in similar market conditions as one goes up, the other goes down). Two stocks that react similarly to market stimuli are said to be positively correlated. Conversely, two stocks that act in opposite ways are said to be inversely (or negatively) correlated. Then there is the matter of being uncorrelated – where two items behave randomly with respect to each other in similar conditions. We can quantify this behavior by a calculation of correlation[2]. Correlation involves two streams of data and the calculated correlation coefficient can range from -1.0 to +1.0. The extremes (-1.0 and +1.0) indicate perfect correlation, while 0 (zero) indicates non-correlation or something that is said to be uncorrelated. The plus sign (+) indicates positive correlation (as one stream of data goes up the other stream of data will tend to go up), whereas the negative sign (-) indicates an inverse (or negative) correlation (as one stream of data goes up the other stream will tend to go down, and vice versa). As we get closer to 0 (zero), we are less and less likely to make an accurate inference about what will happen to one stream of data given that we know what happened to the other. The closer we get to 1, the more accurate our inference about what will happen to a stream of data, given that we know what happens to the other stream.

Strong correlation should not imply cause and effect. Because two streams of data are highly correlated, does not mean that one is causing the other. In a test of variables for the purpose of predicting elementary school reading proficiency, it was found that shoe size was the best predictor of a student's reading level. As it turns out, the best predictor would have been age (at the elementary school level the older you are, generally the better the reader you are). But age was somehow left off the list of variables. Shoe size served as a proxy for age. So while shoe size was correlated with reading level, it was not a "cause." And it also was not the case that reading well caused large feet.

Sometimes there is cause and effect, but only in one direction (uni-directionally). There is a high negative correlation between temperature and people wearing heavy coats - the lower the temperature, the heavier the coat. In this case temperature does cause the wearing of the warm outerwear. However,

---

[2]I am providing the formula for Pearson's Product Moment Correlation Coefficient from Excel:

$$r = \frac{\sum (x - \bar{x})(y - \bar{y})}{\sqrt{\sum (x - \bar{x})^2 \sum (y - \bar{y})^2}}$$

18

the opposite is not true – it does not get cold because people wear coats. If it did, then we could have summer year-round by refusing to wear coats.

If we found that the two stocks did tend to behave similarly in varying market conditions, we would want to find another stock to add to the portfolio to add diversification. We would keep adding stocks that contributed to this diversification. Diversification has its limits, though this is not often acknowledged. If we only had two stocks and they were perfectly uncorrelated, it would be like flipping a coin to determine the return for one stock given that we know the return of the other. As someone tried to explain to me, "Maybe when investors say they want uncorrelated investments, they mean when everything goes up they want this investment to go up, and when everything goes down they want this investment to go up." Of course, as I pointed out, they would have invested in something that never went down and who wouldn't want that.

There is no accepted standard of what level of correlation is associated with which descriptive term. I will use the following scheme:

Uncorrelated:	Absolute value 0.0 to .19
Slight correlation:	Absolute value .20 to .39
Moderate correlation:	Absolute value .40 to .59
High correlation:	Absolute value .60 to .79
Extreme correlation:	Absolute value .80 to 1.00

What We Know: Long-term correlation is a useful metric

This must be true, because fund managers usually provide only long-term correlation data, generally in the range of a 15 – 20 year correlation calculation (or as long as their fund has been around, if less). Whereas they provide investment returns for multiple, shorter, recent periods (1-month, 3-month, 6-month, 1-year, 3-year, 5-year, etc.) but the correlation calculation is often for a single, long-term period.

Correlation can confuse even those that understand it, especially when talking about uncorrelated investments. I can think of many instances where people have confused negative correlation with non-correlation. A correlation of -1.0 is exactly the same strength of a relationship as +1.0, just in an inverse way. Non-correlation is centered around a calculated correlation of 0.0 (and spanning from -.19 to +.19, according to my definition of what constitutes the range of non-correlation) the most uncorrelated that two streams of data can be. Figure 1 is a scenario where the correlation is 0.0[3]:

Figure 1
Uncorrelated Streams

Observation	X	Y
1	1	1
2	2	2
3	3	3
4	4	4
5	5	5
6	5	6
7	4	7
8	3	8
9	2	9
10	1	10

An investor that selected these two stocks, because they wanted two uncorrelated investments, would be quite pleased that they have two investments that are perfectly uncorrelated with each other. Looking closer though, we see that what the investor has actually added to the portfolio are two investments that are either perfectly positively correlated or perfectly negatively correlated. If we take the correlation of the first 5 observations we get 1.0 and if we take the correlation of the last 5 observations we get -1.0. Taken as a whole, the correlation is 0.0, but broken down into two subsets we see a different reality.

Any long-term correlation calculation can be broken down into shorter periods. When correlation is calculated over a long time frame, this long term correlation is actually comprised of a number of shorter periods of any desired length. An investor that hoped to add uncorrelated investments to the portfolio and relied on the long-term correlation calculation might possibly be adding investments to their portfolio that, in the short-term, were highly correlated with the streams that were used to calculate the

---

[3]The origin of this example stems from a paper I wrote with my colleague Andrew (Andy) Braunstein, "Correlation of Uncorrelated Asset Classes," *The Journal of International Business and Economy*, Volume 9, Issue 2, December 2008, pp 1-12

correlation statistic. Typically, correlation between individual investments (and asset classes) is calculated using the extended time periods.

To get a sense about whether there was shorter, highly correlated rolling periods within longer uncorrelated series, I used two series of 180 random numbers representing 15 years of monthly returns[4]. Random numbers seemed like a reasonable choice for a data set since uncorrelated streams behave randomly relative to each other. The correlation of the two series was taken, tested as uncorrelated as it should, since they were two sets of random numbers. Correlations were then taken in 12-month rolling periods (which amounted to 169 such rolling periods). A test of statistical significance of the 12-month rolling correlations was performed at various significance levels. This procedure was repeated 110 times.

The absolute value of the overall correlations was less than .05 in 53% of the trials and from .05 to less than .10 in 31% of the trials. Thus, 84% of the trials had overall correlations below .10. Additionally, all overall correlations were below .20 (meeting my definition of uncorrelated). While the paper went through the significance levels and provided more details, I won't bore you with those. At a significance level of .10, observations (meaning the rolling 12-month correlations) were significant 15% of the time. The inescapable conclusion was that within each trial of two sets of 180 uncorrelated numbers, there will be 12-month rolling correlations that are significant. While it can be said that over the long term (15 years) the two series are not correlated, the same cannot be said for the short term (12 months).

Even though the 15- year uncorrelated data contained significant 12-month correlations, what concerns the investor is what the correlation will be next month and into the future, not what it has been over an extended period or even for a 12-month rolling period where that 12-month period may have happened 10 years ago. This is also true for investment returns. Since there is no ability to predict the future for either returns or correlations, at least with returns there is also data presented for shorter, recent periods. The underlying concern is that a 15-year correlation that is low might obscure more recent data by virtue of the length of time used in the correlation calculation.

---

[4]This also comes from that paper I wrote with Andy Braunstein, "Correlation of Uncorrelated Asset Classes."

With the results from looking at the 12-month rolling correlations buried within the longer term uncorrelated streams, I decided to alter the test in two ways. First, I wanted to see if there would be longer periods of high correlation embedded within the long term uncorrelated data streams, and second, I also wanted to look at the last 36, 24 and 12 months of the 180-month data stream. Since the investor is concerned about what the effect is of adding a particular item to the portfolio tomorrow, next month, and perhaps next year, the most recent observations in the streams would seem to be the most relevant.

I again used two series of random numbers (180 observations to simulate 15 years of monthly returns) and ran a short (100 trial) Monte Carlo simulation[5]. High correlations of the shorter, recent periods would suggest that portfolio construction based on extended period correlations should also be looked at using the more recent correlations, since this is what the portfolio effect would be. Further, as often as asset allocations are rebalanced, the correlations should be rebalanced as well because strategies, personnel, etc. change over time.

The correlation of the two series was obtained, which was close to zero, as expected, since sets of random numbers should be uncorrelated. Correlations were then taken for the last 36, 24 and 12 months of the series, since this is the closest representation of the effect that will be introduced into the portfolio. In other words, the relevant correlation is the most recent one, not one that happened 15 years ago. I then performed 100 iterations.

Each of the 100 trials had an overall correlation of less than .20 (meeting my definition of non-correlated). When I looked at the correlations of the last 36, 24 and 12 months, some interesting results appear. When looking at the last 36 months of each trial, 27% of the time (27/100) the correlation was .20 or more, 9% of the time the correlation was .30 or more, and 2% of the time the correlation was .40 or more.

For the last 24 months, a correlation of .20 or more occurred 33% of the time, a correlation of .30 or more occurred 18% of the time, a correlation of

[5]This comes from a paper I wrote with Andy Braunstein, "Examining the Role of Short-Term Correlation in Portfolio Diversification," *Graziado Business Report*, 2009, Volume 12, Issue 3.

.40 or more occurred 6% of the time, and a correlation of .50 or more occurred 2% of the time.

The last 12 months might be the most relevant time frame because this represents the most likely effect on a portfolio. A correlation of .20 or more occurred 61% of the time, a correlation of .30 or more occurred 39% of the time, a correlation of .40 or more occurred 21% of the time and a correlation of .50 or more occurred 10% of the time. An investor adding an investment and expecting it to be uncorrelated (based on 15 years worth of data) could very well be surprised at the resultant effect.

If an investor is adding an investment to a portfolio with the hope that this investment will provide diversification, then there is a need to carefully parse the overall correlation into shorter, more recent metrics. The nearer and shorter the time period, the greater the likelihood the correlation will move from uncorrelated to correlated. Since the correlation to be added to the portfolio is more related to the 180th month than the 1st month of the series, the additional calculation of a near term 36, 24 and 12 month correlation could prove useful.

I believe that the use of extended period correlations can lead to erroneous decisions about how investments will perform once added to a portfolio, at least in the near term. It would remain to be seen whether the investment will live up to its uncorrelated claim over a longer period. It seems to me that investors should request, and fund managers should provide, shorter term correlations along with the longer term, similarly (but not exactly) as they do with returns.

What We Know: You can only use returns when calculating correlation

I found that people, especially quantitative finance professionals and academics, react strongly to the question of whether to use prices (net asset values or NAVs) or returns when calculating correlation. The quants and academics will say that you can ONLY use returns because prices are non-stationary and non-independent. (I am not sure if they are correct about the first part, about only using returns, but they are correct about the second part, that prices are non-stationary and non-independent.)

I do understand the statistical underpinnings and the desirability of the data to possess stationarity and independence. But, I also think that the statistical shortcomings of price streams may not magically be countered by the translation from price to return. (Returns are derived from prices by subtracting the prior period's price from this period's price then dividing by the prior period's price). Some people thought that if you took a pile of bad mortgages, grouped them together and renamed them, then they were no longer a bad investment. Returns are derivative of prices – it is hard to escape that nothing magical happens in a transformation from price to return.

Figure 2 shows two streams of data comprising 120 observations and representing 10 years of monthly prices. The correlation of the two streams is 1.0, perfectly correlated. This is not surprising since, of the 120 observations, 119 are exactly the same (the one difference is highlighted).

Next, I calculated the returns of these two streams (Figure 3). There are 119 observations of which 117 are exactly the same (the two differences are highlighted). The correlation is .00, perfectly uncorrelated.

I cannot tell you which of the two correlation calculations are superior – the one that used prices or the one that used returns. I can say that a reasonable person looking at the data might agree that in both cases there seems to be a high correlation (even a really, really high correlation). I would suggest that to issue a blanket disregard for the use of the prices in calculating correlation is wrong. The use of returns can withstand certain statistical diagnostic tests that the use of prices would fail, but this should not trump common sense.

Figure 2
Correlation of Prices (NAVs)

Obs	A	B	Obs	A	B	Obs	A	B
1	100	100	41	704	704	81	4,956	4,956
2	105	105	42	739	739	82	5,204	5,204
3	110	110	43	776	776	83	5,464	5,464
4	116	116	44	815	815	84	5,737	5,737
5	122	122	45	856	856	85	6,024	6,024
6	128	128	46	899	899	86	6,325	6,325
7	134	134	47	943	943	87	6,642	6,642
8	141	141	48	991	991	88	6,974	6,974
9	148	148	49	1,040	1,040	89	7,322	7,322
10	155	155	50	1,092	1,092	90	7,689	4,900
11	163	163	51	1,147	1,147	91	8,073	8,073
12	171	171	52	1,204	1,204	92	8,477	8,477
13	180	180	53	1,264	1,264	93	8,900	8,900
14	189	189	54	1,327	1,327	94	9,346	9,346
15	198	198	55	1,394	1,394	95	9,813	9,813
16	208	208	56	1,464	1,464	96	10,303	10,303
17	218	218	57	1,537	1,537	97	10,818	10,819
18	229	229	58	1,614	1,614	98	11,360	11,360
19	241	241	59	1,694	1,694	99	11,927	11,927
20	253	253	60	1,779	1,779	100	12,524	12,524
21	265	265	61	1,868	1,868	101	13,150	13,150
22	279	279	62	1,961	1,961	102	13,808	13,808
23	293	293	63	2,059	2,059	103	14,498	14,498
24	307	307	64	2,162	2,162	104	15,223	15,223
25	323	323	65	2,270	2,270	105	15,984	15,984
26	339	339	66	2,384	2,384	106	16,783	16,783
27	356	356	67	2,503	2,503	107	17,622	17,622
28	373	373	68	2,628	2,628	108	18,503	18,503
29	392	392	69	2,760	2,760	109	19,429	19,429
30	412	412	70	2,898	2,898	110	20,400	20,400
31	432	432	71	3,043	3,043	111	21,420	21,420
32	454	454	72	3,195	3,195	112	22,491	22,491
33	476	476	73	3,355	3,355	113	23,616	23,616
34	500	500	74	3,522	3,522	114	24,796	24,796
35	525	525	75	3,698	3,698	115	26,036	26,036
36	552	552	76	3,883	3,883	116	27,338	27,338
37	579	579	77	4,077	4,077	117	28,705	28,705
38	608	608	78	4,281	4,281	118	30,140	30,140
39	639	639	79	4,495	4,495	119	31,647	31,647
40	670	670	80	4,720	4,720	120	33,230	33,230
						Correlation		1.00

Figure 3
Correlation of Returns

Obs	A	B	Obs	A	B	Obs	A	B
			40	0.05	0.05	80	0.05	0.05
1	0.05	0.05	41	0.05	0.05	81	0.05	0.05
2	0.05	0.05	42	0.05	0.05	82	0.05	0.05
3	0.05	0.05	43	0.05	0.05	83	0.05	0.05
4	0.05	0.05	44	0.05	0.05	84	0.05	0.05
5	0.05	0.05	45	0.05	0.05	85	0.05	0.05
6	0.05	0.05	46	0.05	0.05	86	0.05	0.05
7	0.05	0.05	47	0.05	0.05	87	0.05	0.05
8	0.05	0.05	48	0.05	0.05	88	0.05	0.05
9	0.05	0.05	49	0.05	0.05	89	0.05	-0.33
10	0.05	0.05	50	0.05	0.05	90	0.05	0.65
11	0.05	0.05	51	0.05	0.05	91	0.05	0.05
12	0.05	0.05	52	0.05	0.05	92	0.05	0.05
13	0.05	0.05	53	0.05	0.05	93	0.05	0.05
14	0.05	0.05	54	0.05	0.05	94	0.05	0.05
15	0.05	0.05	55	0.05	0.05	95	0.05	0.05
16	0.05	0.05	56	0.05	0.05	96	0.05	0.05
17	0.05	0.05	57	0.05	0.05	97	0.05	0.05
18	0.05	0.05	58	0.05	0.05	98	0.05	0.05
19	0.05	0.05	59	0.05	0.05	99	0.05	0.05
20	0.05	0.05	60	0.05	0.05	100	0.05	0.05
21	0.05	0.05	61	0.05	0.05	101	0.05	0.05
22	0.05	0.05	62	0.05	0.05	102	0.05	0.05
23	0.05	0.05	63	0.05	0.05	103	0.05	0.05
24	0.05	0.05	64	0.05	0.05	104	0.05	0.05
25	0.05	0.05	65	0.05	0.05	105	0.05	0.05
26	0.05	0.05	66	0.05	0.05	106	0.05	0.05
27	0.05	0.05	67	0.05	0.05	107	0.05	0.05
28	0.05	0.05	68	0.05	0.05	108	0.05	0.05
29	0.05	0.05	69	0.05	0.05	109	0.05	0.05
30	0.05	0.05	70	0.05	0.05	110	0.05	0.05
31	0.05	0.05	71	0.05	0.05	111	0.05	0.05
32	0.05	0.05	72	0.05	0.05	112	0.05	0.05
33	0.05	0.05	73	0.05	0.05	113	0.05	0.05
34	0.05	0.05	74	0.05	0.05	114	0.05	0.05
35	0.05	0.05	75	0.05	0.05	115	0.05	0.05
36	0.05	0.05	76	0.05	0.05	116	0.05	0.05
37	0.05	0.05	77	0.05	0.05	117	0.05	0.05
38	0.05	0.05	78	0.05	0.05	118	0.05	0.05
39	0.05	0.05	79	0.05	0.05	119	0.05	0.05
						Correlation		0.00

If you feel that there is something contrived about the examples, you are correct. This data is certainly artificial. Real data is messy – you cannot ordinarily look at any extended period of monthly returns and make a judgment decision about whether the streams are correlated or not. This example allows the reader to look at the streams and come to a reasoned decision about whether they are correlated and to what extent. The calculation of correlation should be robust enough to work in a contrived environment as well as with real-time, actual data[6].

After seeing this result, I got curious about whether the same effect would be observed when varying the different elements:
-shorter time periods
-whether the change occurred early in the sequence, in the middle or towards the end
-changing the constant increase to a constant rate of increase

For shorter time periods, I started with a basic data set comprised of two streams of data (20 observations) where the value of observation 1 is set at 100[7]. Each period the value increases by 10 and this continues for each of the next 19 periods, such that at the end of the 20th period the value has become 290 in each case. I then calculate a return for each period, so that 19 returns are calculated. Since the prices and returns are exactly the same in the streams, the correlation of price and the correlation of return is each 1.0.

From this basic data set variables are manipulated and the correlation of prices is taken as well as the correlation of returns. The first variation is to change the value of one observation in one stream early in the sequence – the fourth observation of one series is changed by lowering the price by 33%. The fifth observation is increased in this stream so that it once again is equal to the fifth observation in the other stream (this increase represents a 75% increase). Of the 20 observations of price, all are the same except for the fourth observation. The returns are the same except for the fourth and fifth observations. The correlation of price is .99 and the correlation of return is .14.

---

[6]I applaud anyone who does not want to take my word for the examples presented and decides to replicate the results. When replicating using a "cut and paste" method for entering data there can be vastly different results than I present.
[7]The actual data sets are provided in the Appendix

The second variation involves incorporating the same decrease as above, except that not just the fifth observation is changed – the difference to be made up is apportioned equally over the remaining observations so that the last observation of the sequences are again equal. This produces different observations between the two streams in observations 4 through 19, and the same values in observations 1, 2, 3 and 20. The correlation of price is .97 and the correlation of return is -.10.

The third variation involves again changing the fourth observation as before. All future observations increase by the standard amount. This variation results in observations 1 – 3 being the same between the two streams and all others (observations 4 – 20) being different. The correlation of price is .96 and the correlation of return is -.11.

Given the very different correlations provided by using prices and returns (extreme correlation for price and slight correlation for return), which is the superior metric? There is no definitive answer, but I would suggest the reader look at the data sets (reproduced in the Appendix) and make their own decision about which correlation seems to better represent the data.

The next set of three variations mirrors the changes of the first three, except that the change is not made in the fourth observation but in observation 12 (and is a 35% drop). The three variations recover the drop in the next observation (variation 4), equally over the remaining observations (variation 5) and increase by a constant amount for the remaining observations (variation 6). The correlation of price and the correlation of returns are:

Variation	Correlation of Price	Correlation of Return
4	.96	-.05
5	.89	.05
6	.76	.21

In the next set of variations (variations 7 – 9), the change is moved toward the end of the sequence (observation 17, a 32% drop). Variation 7 involves recapturing the drop in the next observation; variation 8 recaptures the drop over the remaining observations and variation 9 increases by a static amount. The correlations are:

Variation	Correlation of Price	Correlation of Return
7	.94	.04
8	.91	.09
9	.78	.39

Variations 10 – 18 repeat the first 9 except, instead of using a static increase to change the price, I use a static return. For each period the increase is set to 5%. In variation 10, the drop occurs in observation 4 and is about a 25% drop. The recovery occurs in observation 5. So for 19 of the 20 observations the prices are the same (one is different) and the returns are the same in all but 2.

In variation 11, the drop occurs again in observation 4 but, the recovery is spread evenly over the remaining observations. In variation 12, the observations after the drop increase by a static return. The correlation of price and the correlation of return are:

Variation	Correlation of Price	Correlation of Return
10	.99	-.32
11	.97	-.30
12	.96	-.28

Variations 13 – 15 follow in similar fashion, moving the drop from the beginning of the sequence to the middle of the sequence, with the drop recovered in one of three manners: in the next observation (variation 13), evenly over the remaining observations (variation 14) or all observations subsequent to the drop increase a static return (variation 15). The correlations are:

Variation	Correlation of Price	Correlation of Return
13	.96	-.09
14	.87	.03
15	.61	-.06

The last set of variations utilizing a short data set involves making the drop toward the end of the sequence. The recoveries follow a similar pattern. The correlations are:

Variation	Correlation of Price	Correlation of Return
16	.93	.10
17	.89	-.03
18	.68	-.11

The next 18 variations recreate the first 18, except with longer data sets (120 observations instead of 20). The correlations are:

Variation	Correlation of Price	Correlation of Return
19	1.00	.30
20	.99	.44
21	.99	.44
22	1.00	.30
23	.98	.48
24	.97	.51
25	1.00	.29
26	.97	.48
27	.92	.52
28	1.00	.08
29	1.00	.08
30	1.00	.08
31	1.00	-.08
32	1.00	-.05
33	1.00	-.06
34	1.00	.03
35	.99	.05
36	.99	.04

While the correlation of price is close to 1.00 in almost all instances, the correlation of return reaches a maximum of .52 and, in most instances, is much less. The correlation of price is extreme whereas the correlation of return tends to be uncorrelated.

The data sets are contained in the Appendix. Figure 4 (for those instances of 20 observations) and Figure 5 (for those instances of 120 observations) summarize the variations and the correlations. The columns in the figures are:

Variation	-the variation number
Figure	-the figure in which the example appears
Panel	-the panel in the figure in which the example appears
Drop	-whether the drop occurs at the beginning, middle or end of the sequence
Recovery	-whether the recovery occurs immediately, evenly over the remaining periods or continues at the standard rate of increase
Increase	-whether the increase is based on a standard price increase (Price) or a standard return increase (Return)
Price	-the correlation of price
Return	-the correlation of return

Based on the examples presented, the correlation of price appears to be more relevant than the correlation of return. Given that an investor might pursue an investment because it is highly correlated (whether positive or negative) or non-correlated, they will rely on the correlation calculation to provide information about the behavior of the investment they want to add to the portfolio, relative to some other data stream. Both streams in all examples tend to move similarly – reflective of a high correlation. The correlation of price produces a high correlation coefficient, whereas, the correlation of return produces a statistic that tends to indicate non-correlation or very little correlation. Looking at the data streams on an individual observation basis, the correlation of price seems to better reflect the behavior of the underlying data.

Another, perhaps more basic rationale, exists for utilizing prices rather than returns. What is being added to the portfolio is the dollar value of the investment, or the price. From the change in price the return is derived. At the end of any period it is the value of the investment that is most important – not the return. Without the price there is no return. The price is what is being put into the portfolio and from that, the return follows.

31

Figure 4
Variations Using 20 Periods

Variation	Appendix	Panel	Drop	Recovery	Increase	Correlation of: Price	Return
1	1	1	Beginning	Immediate	Price	.99	.14
2	1	2	Beginning	Over remaining	Price	.97	-.10
3	1	3	Beginning	Standard Increase	Price	.96	-.11
4	2	1	Middle	Immediate	Price	.96	.05
5	2	2	Middle	Over remaining	Price	.89	.05
6	2	3	Middle	Standard Increase	Price	.76	.21
7	3	1	End	Immediate	Price	.94	.04
8	3	2	End	Over remaining	Price	.91	.09
9	3	3	End	Standard Increase	Price	.78	.39
10	4	1	Beginning	Immediate	Return	.99	-.32
11	4	2	Beginning	Over remaining	Return	.97	-.30
12	4	3	Beginning	Standard Increase	Return	.96	-.28
13	5	1	Middle	Immediate	Return	.96	-.09
14	5	2	Middle	Over remaining	Return	.87	.03
15	5	3	Middle	Standard Increase	Return	.61	-.06
16	6	1	End	Immediate	Return	.93	.10
17	6	2	End	Over remaining	Return	.89	-.03
18	6	3	End	Standard Increase	Return	.68	-.11

Figure 5
Variations Using 120 Periods

Variation	Appendix	Panel	Drop	Recovery	Increase	Correlation of: Price	Return
19	7	1	Beginning	Immediate	Price	1.00	.30
20	7	2	Beginning	Over remaining	Price	.99	.44
21	7	3	Beginning	Standard increase	Price	.99	.44
22	8	1	Middle	Immediate	Price	1.00	.30
23	8	2	Middle	Over remaining	Price	.98	.48
24	8	3	Middle	Standard increase	Price	.97	.51
25	9	1	End	Immediate	Price	1.00	.29
26	9	2	End	Over remaining	Price	.97	.48
27	9	3	End	Standard increase	Price	.92	.52
28	10	1	Beginning	Immediate	Return	1.00	.08
29	10	2	Beginning	Over remaining	Return	1.00	.08
30	10	3	Beginning	Standard increase	Return	1.00	.08
31	11	1	Middle	Immediate	Return	1.00	-.08
32	11	2	Middle	Over remaining	Return	1.00	-.05
33	11	3	Middle	Standard increase	Return	1.00	-.06
34	12	1	End	Immediate	Return	1.00	.03
35	12	2	End	Over remaining	Return	.99	.05
36	12	3	End	Standard increase	Return	.99	.04

-2-
THE MARKET GOES TO 1

In periods of market turmoil, it can often be heard that the "market goes to 1", which usually implies that all investment choices are moving in the same direction (down). For anyone involved in the financial industry, whether by direct job function or by tangential relationship, the period that started in the fall of 2007 represented an interesting time. And when an academic (or medical professional) uses the term "interesting", it seldom means something good - interesting usually means something anomalous, out of the ordinary, strange. What was a bull market of admirable length became a pile of devastation – all returns refunded, as well as principal (and principle), receding to levels not seen in many years (and careers).

It does bring up two questions – the first question, how likely is it that the market can go to 1, and the second question, did the market go to 1? What these questions refer to is the metric of correlation and the relationship of two streams of data. In an investment context, correlation is applied to the return series of two investments (or asset classes). Despite the previous chapter, where I argue that prices (possibly) should be used over returns (and I still think at times they should), in this chapter to answer these questions, I use returns because that is what was used by those that say the market went to 1.

When it is said that the market goes to 1, what is really meant is that all investment choices are moving in the same direction – downward. Not surprisingly, in the period up to mid-2007 it could have been said that the market went to 1, but in a positive direction. Everything was going up and there were few bad investments. For sure, some did better than others, but all seemed to do well. Investment professionals do not focus on this because that would remove their acumen from their returns – when everything is going up it is their skill, when everything is going down it is because the market went to 1.

In order to ponder about whether the market went to 1 there are two conditions precedent that must be considered:
- what constitutes the market and
- what level of correlation is close enough to be considered 1

Certainly, when we say the market went to 1, we mean that different asset classes had an extreme level of correlation simultaneously. No one takes this claim at a literal level – that is, that all asset classes had to have a correlation of exactly 1 simultaneously. Since there is no accepted threshold of what correlation is high enough to be considered 1, I would suggest that .80 (and above) is a good cutoff for a surrogate of a correlation of 1. Everyone can make their own assessment of what level is close enough to 1. In my suggested nomenclature I said that I consider extreme correlation to occur at .80 and above, so consistency dictates I continue with that threshold for determination of what is a high enough correlation for us to say that the two streams were at 1.

The question of what constitutes "the market" could be tougher to answer. At this point, I am suggesting that six asset classes constitute the market. It doesn't really matter what six asset classes you use (it will later on, but not right now), just that you accept that six asset classes comprise the "market." The only real trouble starts if you consider less than six asset classes to constitute the market. Less than six asset classes could result in a different outcome than I found – but if you think that the market is comprised of more than six asset classes my results are still valid.

What we know: In times of market stress, the correlation of all asset classes goes to 1

Since correlation is typically presented using an extended (15-year) time-frame, I first wondered what effect a recent phenomena (market crash) would have on the long-term correlation – does twelve months of extreme correlation have any effect on 180 months of low correlation? Would a recent total market collapse, which caused the market to go to 1 for some period of time, provide a correlation over the last 15 years (including this period of extreme correlation) that approaches a significant relationship, given that there was low correlation previously, when calculated over the extended duration?

36

So why not take 180 observations of two streams of uncorrelated returns and replace the last twelve observations of one stream so that the last twelve observations of each stream were equal. In this way, we have 168 months of uncorrelated returns followed by 12 months (the last 12 months of the 180-month series) of perfectly correlated returns.

I utilized two streams of 180 random numbers representing the returns of two investments over 15 years[8]. I then set the last twelve observations of each stream equal, representing perfect correlation of the last twelve observations and took the correlation over the 15 years (where the first 168 observations were random and the last 12 set equal). I repeated this 100 times.

I then went back and set the last 18 observations equal (changing an additional 6 from the paragraph above) and repeated the process 100 times. I then set the last 24 observations equal (again, changing an additional 6) and repeated 100 times. The following (Figure 6) represents the results obtained:

Figure 6
Correlation with the Last 12, 18, 24 Observations Set Equal

Range of Correlation		N Number of Last Observations Set Equal		
From	To	12	18	24
.00	.04	28	23	10
.05	.09	37	28	26
.10	.14	24	28	23
.15	.19	10	12	21
.20	.24	1	6	14
.25	.29	0	2	5
.30	.34	0	1	0
.35	.39	0	0	0
.40	.45	0	0	1
Total		100	100	100

---

[8]This comes from a paper I wrote, "Does the Market Go to 1?" *The Journal of Business and Economics Research*, Volume 8, Number 3, March 2010, pp 99-102.

When the last 12 observations were set equal (representing a year of the market at 1), a correlation of greater than .20 (but less than .25) happened 1% of the time (once). A correlation equal to or greater than .15 and less than .20 happened 10% of the time (10 times) and a correlation equal to or greater than .10 and less than .15 happened 24% of the time (24 times). No correlation was above .25.

When the last 18 observations are set equal (representing a year and a half of perfect correlation), a correlation equal to or greater than .30 and less than .35 was observed 1% of the time (once). A correlation equal to or greater than .25 and less than .30 was observed 2% of the time (twice) and a correlation equal to or greater than .20 and less than .25, 6% of the time (6 times).

Now when the last 24 observations are set equal (representing two years of perfect correlation), a correlation equal to or greater than .40 and less than .45 occurred 1% of the time (once). No correlation was above .45. So if we accept that long term correlations are low, chances are that the last 12/18/24 months (when set to a correlation of 1) do not make the original data set extreme, high or even moderately correlated.

It is for each reader to decide at what level correlation (and non-correlation) starts to exist. To me, non-correlation exists at and below .19 and a slight relationship begins from .20 and runs to .39. A moderate correlation goes from .40 to .59 and the streams start to get correlated from .60 to .79 (high correlation) and extremely correlated from .80 to 1.0. Nothing presented in this test approaches that.

This first test concerned two streams of data, whereas a true "market going to 1" includes more than two streams of data. For the second test, I utilized six streams of data (each stream was 180 observations, representing 15 years of monthly returns) which represents six broad (but unspecified) asset classes (that, taken together, would constitute the market). The random monthly returns used parameters that allowed them to go from -50 to +50, simulating high monthly return volatility. Taking the six asset classes two at a time, you wind up with 15 simultaneous correlation calculations. In a true "market to 1" scenario, all 15 calculations have to be highly correlated simultaneously.

In this test I looked at rolling three month periods, so that during the 15 years (180 months), I was looking for any consecutive three month period where all six streams were highly correlated. For each run there were 178 chances for the six streams to be highly correlated. I ran this 100 times.

Allowing for different thresholds of what level of correlation is considered "being at 1," I present the results for three levels (correlation values of .70, .80 or a .90). Figure 7 contains the number of times and the percentage that the three month rolling correlation achieved the specified level of correlation.

Figure 7
Three Month Rolling Correlation

	Absolute value of correlation		
	> .70	> .80	> .90
Number observed	119	34	6
Percentage of total	0.67%	0.19%	0.03%

There were 17,800 chances for all 15 correlations to be above a certain threshold (100 runs x 178 rolling three- month periods). At the .90 level this happened 6 times, at the .80 level, 34 times and at the .70 level, 119 times. The test was somewhat unrealistic in a number of senses:
- the recent market turmoil happened during the last three months, while this test looks at any three months
- the test looks at the absolute value of correlations, which could mean that some high correlations were negative and some were positive (we would only be concerned with positive correlation in a "market to 1" scenario)
- the parameters were constant and symmetric throughout the 180 observations, whereas it is more likely that the range became asymmetric during the period of turmoil – perhaps using a range from - 50 to +20 during the period of turmoil would have been more realistic
- the test was also less restrictive in only using a rolling three-month period. Sustained periods of financial distress are usually longer than three months.

The test had relaxed certain characteristics of a true "market to 1." Instead of being the last three months (the most recent period), the test included any three months (which increased the possibility of occurrence from once per run to 178 per run). The test also looked at the absolute value of returns instead of only the positively correlated ones. The test used a consistent range of monthly returns (-50 to +50), whereas the range could have been asymmetric (say -50 to +20). And lastly, the test used a rolling period of three months, instead of a more reasonable six to nine (or twelve or twenty-four, your pick) month period.

Given the parameters used to conduct the test, my conclusion is that the market can go to 1. Though certainly a rare occurrence, the test indicates it can happen (albeit in only .0003 of the observations). It can happen, but most likely doesn't happen. For discussions of six-sigma events and whether they are good bets, I refer the reader to do an internet search on "Long Term Capital Management."

Moving from the abstract (can the market go to 1) to the concrete (did the "market go to 1") there is a succinct answer – no, it did not. US Government securities were uncorrelated with the rest of the market, so the question has a ready answer. So, I re-phrase the question to "did the market go to 1 holding US Government Securities aside?"

Since I will be looking at actual data and not using random numbers, it is not enough to say that market consists of six asset classes – they must be delineated (as promised, the time has come). At a basic level, there are equity and debt markets. However, within the equity and debt markets, there are sub-classes of domestic and international markets, along with developed and emerging markets. Within the domestic equity markets, there are large cap, mid cap, small cap and within these, growth and value subsets. Within the domestic debt markets, there are corporate and government sectors, plus others. There are many ways to further sub-divide any of those markets. In addition to the myriad choices as to how to divide the equity and debt markets, there are also commodities, hard assets and real estate and alternative assets to consider. I chose a limited, but representative number of asset classes to constitute the market. While it certainly is not all encompassing, if the market did not go to 1 with the limited set of choices used here, then there is no benefit to expanding the number of asset classes – the market will still not have gone to 1. The reader should feel free to disagree with my choices of representative asset classes.

At a top level, the equity markets can be broken down into developed and emerging markets and within developed markets, into domestic and international ones. This provides three basic, broad equity markets – US, developed international and emerging. To provide return streams, I used indices and for expediency, the ETFs (exchange-traded funds) built on specific indices. Choosing ETFs that had high tracking error to the underlying indices would have confounded the results. I believe that the choices made are reasonable surrogates for the "true" market returns. In some cases, I chose more than one index for an asset class. I used the period December 2007 through March 2009 as the duration of the financial crisis.

Equity Market Correlations

The equity indices used for developed markets are as follows:
Domestic equity - S&P 500 and the US Market Index
Developed international - a global index (SPDR DJ Global Titans) and an all-world index not including the US (Vanguard FTSE All World ex-US)

The reader is free to disagree about the number and choice of asset classes, as well as the use of ETF indices. The correlation matrix is shown in Figure 8.

Figure 8
Equity Market Correlation Matrix

	S&P 500	US Market Index	SPDR DJ Global Titans	Vanguard FTSE All World ex-US
S&P 500	1.000	0.997	0.969	0.930
US Market Index		1.000	0.968	0.940
SPDR DJ Global Titans			1.000	0.955
Vanguard FTSE All World ex-US				1.000

The correlations are extremely high. At an overall market level, it is a reasonable conclusion that the domestic (US) and international developed equity markets were at 1 during this time period.

Emerging Market Correlations

Adding a broad emerging market equity index (Vanguard Emerging Markets Stock Index) as an additional asset class, yields the correlation matrix shown in Figure 9.

Figure 9
Equity Market and Emerging Market Correlation Matrix

	S&P 500	US Market Index	SPDR DJ Global Titans	Vanguard FTSE All World ex-US	Vanguard Emerging Markets Stock
S&P 500	1.000	0.997	0.969	0.930	0.657
US Market Index		1.000	0.968	0.940	0.655
SPDR DJ Global Titans			1.000	0.955	0.701
Vanguard FTSE All World ex-US				1.000	0.660
Vanguard Emerging Markets Stock					1.000

Given the established cutoff value of .80 as representing "being at 1," one would be led to conclude that the emerging equity markets were not "at 1" with either of the developed equity markets. Certainly, one who chooses a somewhat lower value as the cutoff could draw a different conclusion.

Commodity Index Correlations

Adding commodities as an asset class (iShares S&P GSCI Commodity Index) provides the correlation matrix shown in Figure 10.

The commodity index value is under .60 in every case – leading to the conclusion that commodities were not "at 1" with either of the developed equity markets and was uncorrelated with emerging equity markets (since that particular correlation coefficient is .20).

Debt Market Correlations

Adding a broad debt market index (Barclays Aggregate) provides the correlations shown in Figure 11.

Figure 10

Equity Market, Emerging Market and Commodity Correlation Matrix

	S&P 500	US Market Index	SPDR DJ Global Titans	Vanguard FTSE All World ex-US	Vanguard Emerging Markets Stock	iShares S&P GSCI Commodity Index
S&P 500	1.000	0.997	0.969	0.930	0.657	0.552
US Market Index		1.000	0.968	0.940	0.655	0.568
SPDR DJ Global Titans			1.000	0.955	0.701	0.483
Vanguard FTSE All World ex-US				1.000	0.660	0.596
Vanguard Emerging Markets Stock					1.000	0.199
iShares S&P GSCI Commodity Index						1.000

Figure 11

Equity Market, Emerging Market, Commodity and Debt Market Correlation Matrix

	S&P 500	US Market Index	SPDR DJ Global Titans	Vanguard FTSE All World ex-US	Vanguard Emerging Markets Stock	iShares S&P GSCI Commodity Index	Barclays Aggregate
S&P 500	1.000	0.997	0.969	0.930	0.657	0.552	0.305
US Market Index		1.000	0.968	0.940	0.655	0.568	0.314
SPDR DJ Global Titans			1.000	0.955	0.701	0.483	0.321
Vanguard FTSE All World ex-US				1.000	0.660	0.596	0.432
Vanguard Emerging Markets Stock					1.000	0.199	0.238
iShares S&P GSCI Commodity Index						1.000	-0.023
Barclays Aggregate							1.000

We see that the correlations are all below .50 (and mostly in the low .30s or below), indicating a low correlation between the debt indices and all pairs of asset classes. Thus, the overall debt market was not correlated with developed equity markets (domestic or international), emerging equity markets, or commodity markets.

Some proponents of the "market to 1" theory believe that government bonds are not an asset class. They consider government bonds to be an alternative to cash (and perhaps even a substitute for cash, depending on maturity), making them strategic, not investment, holdings. In that case, it is possible that correlations for the broad debt market index would be distorted by the inclusion of government bonds. To investigate further, two other debt indices were added to the matrix – a pure 10-20 year government bond index (iShares Barclays 10-20 Year Government Bond) and a corporate bond index (iShares Barclays Credit Fund). The correlations are shown in Figure 12.

Both the government bond index and the credit index were highly correlated with the aggregate index (Barclays Aggregate), but neither was correlated with the equity (developed or emerging) or commodity indices. As expected, the government bond index had the lowest correlations with the other indices. The credit index had higher, but still low, correlations with the other indices.

The analysis indicates that it is not accurate to say that the "market went to 1" during the financial crisis. Even though many likely felt that such was the case at the time, examination of the correlations throughout the duration of the crisis indicates that the market was not at 1. The developed equity markets (domestic and international) went to 1, but the commodities market and debt market (even separating out the corporate market) did not. Based on the criterion, the emerging equities market did not go to 1, although a lowering of the cutoff point for what constitutes being at 1 could alter that conclusion.

Emerging equity markets are less correlated with developed equity markets, falling slightly below what would be considered extreme correlation, based on the standard of .80 used. For the purposes of asset allocation, however, an investor may still consider a correlation greater than .60 to be significant, even if it does not constitute "going to 1."

During the financial crisis, fixed income (debt) was not correlated with the equity markets (either government or corporate). Fixed income was a diversifier during the sixteen months that the crisis lasted (based on how I define the term of the crisis - some might utilize a different beginning and ending point for the duration of the financial crisis).

Commodities offered returns which were not highly correlated with the returns of equities and were even less so with those of bonds (whether corporate or government). When compared to any other return stream used in this chapter, commodities could be expected to provide uncorrelated returns during periods of financial stress.

Figure 12
Equity Market, Emerging Market, Commodity, Broad Debt, Government Debt and Corporate Debt Market Correlation Matrix

	S&P 500	US Market Index	SPDR DJ Global Titans	Vanguard FTSE All World ex-US	Vanguard Emerging Markets Stock	iShares S&P GSCI Commodity Index	Barclays Aggregate	iShares Barclays 10-20 Yr Gov't Bond	iShares Barclays Credit Fund
S&P 500	1.000	0.997	0.969	0.930	0.657	0.552	0.305	0.249	0.423
US Market Index		1.000	0.968	0.940	0.655	0.568	0.314	0.244	0.447
SPDR DJ Global Titans			1.000	0.955	0.701	0.483	0.321	0.306	0.406
Vanguard FTSE All World ex-US				1.000	0.660	0.596	0.432	0.381	0.541
Vanguard Emerging Markets Stock					1.000	0.199	0.238	0.121	0.302
iShares S&P GSCI Commodity Index						1.000	-0.023	-0.120	0.151
Barclays Aggregate							1.000	0.898	0.865
iShares Barclays 10-20 Year Gov't Bond								1.000	0.615
iShares Barclays Credit Fund									1.000

-3-
<u>DIVERSIFICATION</u>

Diversification is the use of varied investments in a portfolio in order to lessen the possibility of negative market events and cycles affecting all the investments, in the same way, simultaneously. Diversification can come in many forms and through many avenues. It is one of the key risk control methods and has been a pervasive concept in portfolio management. You could own ten different stocks in ten different industry sectors located in ten different countries and consider that diversification. In some respects it is. But since they are all equity securities, there is a characteristic of the investments that are not diversified.

Asset allocation is the first level of diversification, but it is not perfect. A lot depends on how the portfolio is divided. For instance, the portfolio might be divided between equities and fixed income, and within equities, further divided between domestic and international. The fixed income allocation might be divided between government and corporate securities. We could get into further detail by dividing domestic equity into large cap, mid cap and small cap, and then into growth and value, and dividing international equity into developed countries, emerging markets and frontier markets; but let's leave it at four asset classes:

> Domestic equity
> International equity
> Government fixed income
> Corporate fixed income

And for the sake of simplicity, let's allocate 25% of our portfolio to each of the four asset classes. Are we diversified? We very well might be, but then again, we might not be. We hold two fundamentally different types of securities (equity and debt), and we have further allocated between geography (domestic and international) and between government and corporate. Holding different types of securities may not lead to diversification – you could own the stock of a particular company and the bonds of the same company, and therefore wind up with similar risk criteria.

You may also own the stock of one company and the bonds of a different company, where the company whose bonds you hold is dependent on a relationship with the company that you hold shares in. For instance, when the automotive Industry had trouble and the stocks took a dive, so did the shares of those suppliers whose revenues were dependent on sales to the auto manufacturers. So in holding the shares of two distinct companies you may feel like you have effectively diversified, but in actuality the returns may move in similar fashion.

There can also be issues with definition – is a company that is based in the US and listed on a US stock exchange a US company? It seems like the company should be classified as part of the domestic allocation. But suppose that company derives all of its revenue from sales in Europe. Is it still a US company or is it more properly classified as part of the international allocation? We can make the same case for a company domiciled abroad and listed on a foreign exchange, but who has all of their sales made in the US. What should be the proper classification for this company?

Correlation can tell us a lot about where the companies should be classified. Since diversification is a risk minimization concept whose function is to group similarly behaving securities together to identify concentrations, asset classes should be based on behavior rather than archaic notions and old definitions.

What we know: Diversification is synonymous with holding uncorrelated investments

In the perfectly uncorrelated portfolio, each investment will behave randomly with respect to each other. The good news is that in a down market the perfectly uncorrelated portfolio may go up, and in a good market the portfolio may go up as well. The bad news is that the opposite is also true – the portfolio may go down in good markets and down in bad markets. Random behavior means that there is no way to predict what will happen.

So why is diversification different than correlation? It would seem that correlation effectively measures diversification. At an asset class level this might be the case. But most investors do not own whole asset classes – they own investments within asset classes. And often individual selections within the asset class do not behave like the asset class as a whole.

Will two managers or investors, both investing in domestic equity, select the stocks of the same company in the same proportions? Not likely. So, the level of diversification may be the same (the allocation to the asset class), the level of correlation won't be. Likewise, two companies in the same asset class (say two companies properly classified as US Equity, Large Cap, Value) may have very different stock performance – even though the investor may not have diversification, they very well might have uncorrelated investments. Correlation is a statistical concept whereas diversification is a descriptive concept.

An investor has to decide which attribute is paramount – diversification or non-correlation. You can hold securities that are:
- diversified and uncorrelated
- diversified and correlated
- not diversified and uncorrelated
- not diversified and correlated

Diversification and correlation look at two separate attributes, and though correlation seems to measure diversification, it really measures something different (though no less important). What an investor should strive for is to hold securities that are both diversified and uncorrelated. Too often the investor settles for one or the other and doesn't achieve either, or worse, fails to recognize what they are getting by making a particular investment.

-4-
"REAL" RETURNS

Most institutional investors (in this chapter we limit the population of institutional investors to endowments and foundations) have an investment policy with a specified target investment return (individuals investing because they need to live on a fixed income might be interested in this chapter as well). This target is usually denoted as a "real X%" return, where the "X%" represents the return needed to provide the anticipated spending (in an endowment) or the government required distribution (in a private foundation) and the "real" portion represents the adjustment necessary to maintain the purchasing power (inflation factor). Often inflation (usually specified as some version of the consumer price index) is used as the "real" component and is additive to the spending/distribution percentage to derive the total target return of the portfolio.

With a goal of perpetuity, it is important for institutional investors to properly invest and budget and control spending. Maintaining the purchasing power of the portfolio is a key consideration as the organization balances longevity with spending, inflation and return.

What we know: The expected inflation rate is additive to the return needed for spending/distribution to get the portfolio's target return

To illustrate, I use a model of a private foundation with a target of a "real 5%" return[9], during a period of time when the relevant inflation factor is 3%. Most organizations would target 8% as the overall return (5% for distribution and 3% for inflation). This hypothetical private foundation has set an operating budget of $25,000,000 in 2010 (calendar year) and a

---

[9]This comes from my paper: Of "Real" Investment Returns, International Journal of Accounting, Information Science and Leadership, Vol. 5(12) May, 2012 pp. 54-64.

portfolio that was valued at $500,000,000 on December 31, 2010. Assume the organization hits the 8% return target right on the head, as well as inflation comes in at exactly 3% and spending was as planned at 5%. The entity would end 2011 with $514,250,000 (the previous portfolio balance of $500,000,000, plus an 8% investment return, less spending of an inflation adjusted $25,750,000 [the previous budget of $25,000,000 plus 3% inflation]). Achieving the goal of an 8% return produced an excess of $14,250,000 above what was needed. This was due to applying the "real" percentage against the entire endowment when inflation only affects the portion being spent.

Projecting this out over 25 years has the balance of the endowment increasing to $975,568,506 at the end of year 25. Essentially what is happening is the purchasing power is being maintained on the entire endowment, not just the portion that will be expended. Figure 13 shows the annual growth of the portfolio. Clearly the target rate of return (8%) is producing returns well in excess of the spending needs. Since inflation relates to spending and the entity is only spending 5% of the endowment value, perhaps the inflation factor should only relate to the portion to be expended (5%). That would make the annual required return:

$$\text{Total Return} = 5\% + (5\% * 3\%) = 5.15\%$$

Adjusting the previous example to use an annual return of 5.15% (instead of the 8%) produces an endowment value of approximately $59,000,000 at the end of year 25 (see Figure 14) – clearly not meeting a goal of perpetuity. Using a return of 5.15%, the portfolio value will decrease each year.

Figure 13
Growth of Endowment

Year	Endowment Balance	Investment Return 8%	Spending	Inflation 3%	Adjusted Spending
0	500,000,000		25,000,000		
1	514,250,000	40,000,000	25,000,000	750,000	25,750,000
2	528,867,500	41,140,000	25,750,000	772,500	26,522,500
3	543,858,725	42,309,400	26,522,500	795,675	27,318,175
4	559,229,703	43,508,698	27,318,175	819,545	28,137,720
5	574,986,227	44,738,376	28,137,720	844,132	28,981,852
6	591,133,818	45,998,898	28,981,852	869,456	29,851,307
7	607,677,677	47,290,705	29,851,307	895,539	30,746,847
8	624,622,639	48,614,214	30,746,847	922,405	31,669,252
9	641,973,120	49,969,811	31,669,252	950,078	32,619,330
10	659,733,060	51,357,850	32,619,330	978,580	33,597,909
11	677,905,858	52,778,645	33,597,909	1,007,937	34,605,847
12	696,494,305	54,232,469	34,605,847	1,038,175	35,644,022
13	715,500,507	55,719,544	35,644,022	1,069,321	36,713,343
14	734,925,804	57,240,041	36,713,343	1,101,400	37,814,743
15	754,770,683	58,794,064	37,814,743	1,134,442	38,949,185
16	775,034,676	60,381,655	38,949,185	1,168,476	40,117,661
17	795,716,260	62,002,774	40,117,661	1,203,530	41,321,191
18	816,812,734	63,657,301	41,321,191	1,239,636	42,560,827
19	838,320,101	65,345,019	42,560,827	1,276,825	43,837,651
20	860,232,929	67,065,608	43,837,651	1,315,130	45,152,781
21	882,544,199	68,818,634	45,152,781	1,354,583	46,507,364
22	905,245,149	70,603,536	46,507,364	1,395,221	47,902,585
23	928,325,099	72,419,612	47,902,585	1,437,078	49,339,663
24	951,771,254	74,266,008	49,339,663	1,480,190	50,819,853
25	975,568,506	76,141,700	50,819,853	1,524,596	52,344,448

Figure 14
Annual Required Return of 5.15%

Year	Endowment Balance	Investment Return 5.15%	Spending	Inflation 3%	Adjusted Spending
0	500,000,000		25,000,000		
1	500,000,000	25,750,000	25,000,000	750,000	25,750,000
2	499,227,500	25,750,000	25,750,000	772,500	26,522,500
3	497,619,541	25,710,216	26,522,500	795,675	27,318,175
4	495,109,227	25,627,406	27,318,175	819,545	28,137,720
5	491,625,501	25,498,125	28,137,720	844,132	28,981,852
6	487,092,907	25,318,713	28,981,852	869,456	29,851,307
7	481,431,345	25,085,285	29,851,307	895,539	30,746,847
8	474,555,807	24,793,714	30,746,847	922,405	31,669,252
9	466,376,101	24,439,624	31,669,252	950,078	32,619,330
10	456,796,561	24,018,369	32,619,330	978,580	33,597,909
11	445,715,737	23,525,023	33,597,909	1,007,937	34,605,847
12	433,026,075	22,954,360	34,605,847	1,038,175	35,644,022
13	418,613,576	22,300,843	35,644,022	1,069,321	36,713,343
14	402,357,432	21,558,599	36,713,343	1,101,400	37,814,743
15	384,129,654	20,721,408	37,814,743	1,134,442	38,949,185
16	363,794,670	19,782,677	38,949,185	1,168,476	40,117,661
17	341,208,905	18,735,426	40,117,661	1,203,530	41,321,191
18	316,220,337	17,572,259	41,321,191	1,239,636	42,560,827
19	288,668,033	16,285,347	42,560,827	1,276,825	43,837,651
20	258,381,656	14,866,404	43,837,651	1,315,130	45,152,781
21	225,180,947	13,306,655	45,152,781	1,354,583	46,507,364
22	188,875,180	11,596,819	46,507,364	1,395,221	47,902,585
23	149,262,589	9,727,072	47,902,585	1,437,078	49,339,663
24	106,129,760	7,687,023	49,339,663	1,480,190	50,819,853
25	59,250,994	5,465,683	50,819,853	1,524,596	52,344,448

The utilization of 5.15% clearly won't meet the organization's needs. An alternative is to utilize a spending rate that is a floating percentage which represents what is needed in any one year (keeping the endowment at a constant $500,000,000 balance). Each year, the target return would increase to meet the increased spending needs. On this basis, the required return in year 25 would be 10.5% (see Figure 15), a non-trivial target. Another way to look at it is to see when the required annual return becomes 8%. This does not happen until year 16. So, for each of the first 15 years the organization would have less of an investment target than they were trying to achieve each year under the additive system, and then they would either need to raise the return target or cut spending. For an entity with perpetuity as one of the goals, 25 years is a short time frame. The required rate of return will only increase and the continued existence (perpetuity) of the entity would be in jeopardy.

If the 8% targeted return produces unnecessary portfolio growth (and may result in excessive risk taking), and using a target comprised of spending and an inflation factor based only on the portion to be expended produces a portfolio that declines each year, and only targeting what is needed for spending produces target rates that are increasingly harder to achieve (at least after you get past year 16), then what alternatives does an institutional investor have to minimize the target return without impacting the operations and longevity of the organization? Clearly there exists a rate between 5.15% and 8% that would meet the dual priorities of the organization (perpetuity and mission fulfillment). Utilizing a rate of 6% would produce a portfolio that starts to decline in year 8 and finishes year 25 with a balance of approximately $259,000,000 (see Figure 16), which I do not think most organizations would view as an acceptable scenario.

Private foundations have a required minimum distribution of 5% of the average portfolio value (this is simplified, but still illustrative). Utilizing an investment return target of 6% and inflation of 3%, the value of the endowment will start to deteriorate in year 8 (see the previous Figure 16), eventually becoming about $259,000,000 in year 25. At the same time, the spending is in excess of the minimum required distribution. The difference between what the organization spent (the qualifying distribution) and what they were required to spend (the required distribution), either has to be made up (if what they spent was less than required) or can be carried forward and used against future required distributions (if what they spent was greater than what was required). By year 25 the entity will have distributed $363,000,000 (see Figure 17) in excess of the required minimum. Excess distributions, while certainly having a positive impact on society, are also counter to perpetual existence.

Figure 15
Required Investment Return to Fund Real Spending

Year	Endowment Balance	Investment Return Required	Spending	Inflation 3%	Adjusted Spending
0	500,000,000		25,000,000		
1	500,000,000	5.2%	25,000,000	750,000	25,750,000
2	500,000,000	5.3%	25,750,000	772,500	26,522,500
3	500,000,000	5.5%	26,522,500	795,675	27,318,175
4	500,000,000	5.6%	27,318,175	819,545	28,137,720
5	500,000,000	5.8%	28,137,720	844,132	28,981,852
6	500,000,000	6.0%	28,981,852	869,456	29,851,307
7	500,000,000	6.1%	29,851,307	895,539	30,746,847
8	500,000,000	6.3%	30,746,847	922,405	31,669,252
9	500,000,000	6.5%	31,669,252	950,078	32,619,330
10	500,000,000	6.7%	32,619,330	978,580	33,597,909
11	500,000,000	6.9%	33,597,909	1,007,937	34,605,847
12	500,000,000	7.1%	34,605,847	1,038,175	35,644,022
13	500,000,000	7.3%	35,644,022	1,069,321	36,713,343
14	500,000,000	7.6%	36,713,343	1,101,400	37,814,743
15	500,000,000	7.8%	37,814,743	1,134,442	38,949,185
16	500,000,000	8.0%	38,949,185	1,168,476	40,117,661
17	500,000,000	8.3%	40,117,661	1,203,530	41,321,191
18	500,000,000	8.5%	41,321,191	1,239,636	42,560,827
19	500,000,000	8.8%	42,560,827	1,276,825	43,837,651
20	500,000,000	9.0%	43,837,651	1,315,130	45,152,781
21	500,000,000	9.3%	45,152,781	1,354,583	46,507,364
22	500,000,000	9.6%	46,507,364	1,395,221	47,902,585
23	500,000,000	9.9%	47,902,585	1,437,078	49,339,663
24	500,000,000	10.2%	49,339,663	1,480,190	50,819,853
25	500,000,000	10.5%	50,819,853	1,524,596	52,344,448

Figure 16
Using an Investment Return of 6%

Year	Endowment Balance	Investment Return 6%	Spending	Inflation 3%	Adjusted Spending
0	500,000,000		25,000,000		
1	504,250,000	30,000,000	25,000,000	750,000	25,750,000
2	507,982,500	30,255,000	25,750,000	772,500	26,522,500
3	511,143,275	30,478,950	26,522,500	795,675	27,318,175
4	513,674,151	30,668,597	27,318,175	819,545	28,137,720
5	515,512,748	30,820,449	28,137,720	844,132	28,981,852
6	516,592,206	30,930,765	28,981,852	869,456	29,851,307
7	516,840,892	30,995,532	29,851,307	895,539	30,746,847
8	516,182,093	31,010,454	30,746,847	922,405	31,669,252
9	514,533,689	30,970,926	31,669,252	950,078	32,619,330
10	511,807,801	30,872,021	32,619,330	978,580	33,597,909
11	507,910,422	30,708,468	33,597,909	1,007,937	34,605,847
12	502,741,025	30,474,625	34,605,847	1,038,175	35,644,022
13	496,192,144	30,164,462	35,644,022	1,069,321	36,713,343
14	488,148,930	29,771,529	36,713,343	1,101,400	37,814,743
15	478,488,680	29,288,936	37,814,743	1,134,442	38,949,185
16	467,080,340	28,709,321	38,949,185	1,168,476	40,117,661
17	453,783,969	28,024,820	40,117,661	1,203,530	41,321,191
18	438,450,181	27,227,038	41,321,191	1,239,636	42,560,827
19	420,919,541	26,307,011	42,560,827	1,276,825	43,837,651
20	401,021,932	25,255,172	43,837,651	1,315,130	45,152,781
21	378,575,884	24,061,316	45,152,781	1,354,583	46,507,364
22	353,387,852	22,714,553	46,507,364	1,395,221	47,902,585
23	325,251,460	21,203,271	47,902,585	1,437,078	49,339,663
24	293,946,695	19,515,088	49,339,663	1,480,190	50,819,853
25	259,239,048	17,636,802	50,819,853	1,524,596	52,344,448

Figure 17
Growth of the Over-Distribution

Year	Endowment Balance	Investment Return 6%	Spending	Inflation 3%	Adjusted Spending	Required Distribution	Over(Under) Distributed	Cumulative
0	500,000,000		25,000,000					
1	504,250,000	30,000,000	25,000,000	750,000	25,750,000	25,106,250	643,750	643,750
2	507,982,500	30,255,000	25,750,000	772,500	26,522,500	25,305,813	1,216,688	1,860,438
3	511,143,275	30,478,950	26,522,500	795,675	27,318,175	25,478,144	1,840,031	3,700,468
4	513,674,151	30,668,597	27,318,175	819,545	28,137,720	25,620,436	2,517,285	6,217,753
5	515,512,748	30,820,449	28,137,720	844,132	28,981,852	25,729,672	3,252,179	9,469,932
6	516,592,206	30,930,765	28,981,852	869,456	29,851,307	25,802,624	4,048,684	13,518,616
7	516,840,892	30,995,532	29,851,307	895,539	30,746,847	25,835,827	4,911,019	18,429,635
8	516,182,093	31,010,454	30,746,847	922,405	31,669,252	25,825,575	5,843,677	24,273,312
9	514,533,689	30,970,926	31,669,252	950,078	32,619,330	25,767,895	6,851,435	31,124,747
10	511,807,801	30,872,021	32,619,330	978,580	33,597,909	25,658,537	7,939,372	39,064,120
11	507,910,422	30,708,468	33,597,909	1,007,937	34,605,847	25,492,956	9,112,891	48,177,011
12	502,741,025	30,474,625	34,605,847	1,038,175	35,644,022	25,266,286	10,377,736	58,554,747
13	496,192,144	30,164,462	35,644,022	1,069,321	36,713,343	24,973,329	11,740,014	70,294,760
14	488,148,930	29,771,529	36,713,343	1,101,400	37,814,743	24,608,527	13,206,216	83,500,977
15	478,488,680	29,288,936	37,814,743	1,134,442	38,949,185	24,165,940	14,783,245	98,284,222
16	467,080,340	28,709,321	38,949,185	1,168,476	40,117,661	23,639,225	16,478,435	114,762,657
17	453,783,969	28,024,820	40,117,661	1,203,530	41,321,191	23,021,608	18,299,583	133,062,240
18	438,450,181	27,227,038	41,321,191	1,239,636	42,560,827	22,305,854	20,254,973	153,317,213
19	420,919,541	26,307,011	42,560,827	1,276,825	43,837,651	21,484,243	22,353,408	175,670,621
20	401,021,932	25,255,172	43,837,651	1,315,130	45,152,781	20,548,537	24,604,244	200,274,865
21	378,575,884	24,061,316	45,152,781	1,354,583	46,507,364	19,489,945	27,017,419	227,292,284
22	353,387,852	22,714,553	46,507,364	1,395,221	47,902,585	18,299,093	29,603,492	256,895,776
23	325,251,460	21,203,271	47,902,585	1,437,078	49,339,663	16,965,983	32,373,680	289,269,456
24	293,946,695	19,515,088	49,339,663	1,480,190	50,819,853	15,479,954	35,339,899	324,609,355
25	259,239,048	17,636,802	50,819,853	1,524,596	52,344,448	13,829,644	38,514,805	363,124,160

Staying with the target return of 6% and an inflation rate of 3%, and superimposing a parameter where the organization will adjust spending periodically so that they are staying close to the cumulative required distribution (taking into account annual over-and-under distributions), there is an opportunity to use a target rate of 6%, meet the cumulative distribution requirements and not cannibalize the endowment.

As the cumulative over-distribution starts to increase, the entity reduces their spending in years 6 and 11 by half of the cumulative over-distribution. This results in a portfolio balance at the end of year 25 of $628,000,000 and a cumulative over-distribution of $8,000,000. This process can be re-created in perpetuity (see Figure 18).

An entity with an investment goal of perpetuity and a "real X% return" that treats the "real" portion and the "X%" portion as additive, might be introducing more risk into the portfolio than is required. Since the "real" portion only applies to the portion of the portfolio that will be spent, not the entire portfolio, the target return can be substantially less than the sum of the two components.

While not the subject of this chapter, how to quantify "real" is another issue. The real portion relates to inflation and maintenance of purchasing power. Many use one of the consumer price indices (CPI) that are available. If the entity is like many non-profits with about 75% of their spending relating to salaries and benefits, a more specific inflation figure could be derived and used. If the entity is a private foundation, where the largest portion of the spending is for grants, then the entity can adjust the "real" percentage on a discretionary basis, as grant amounts (or the number of grants to be made) tend not to be inflation adjusted, but entity controlled.

Figure 18

Spending Adjusted for Over-Distribution (in Years 6, 11)

Year	Endowment Balance	Investment Return 6%	Spending	Inflation 3%	Adjusted Spending	Required Distribution	Over(Under) Distributed	Cumulative
0	500,000,000							
1	504,250,000	30,000,000	25,000,000	750,000	25,750,000	25,106,250	643,750	643,750
2	507,982,500	30,255,000	25,750,000	772,500	26,522,500	25,305,813	1,216,688	1,860,438
3	511,143,275	30,478,950	26,522,500	795,675	27,318,175	25,478,144	1,840,031	3,700,468
4	513,674,151	30,668,597	27,318,175	819,545	28,137,720	25,620,436	2,517,285	6,217,753
5	515,512,748	30,820,449	28,137,720	844,132	28,981,852	25,729,672	3,252,179	9,469,932
6	521,327,172	30,930,765	28,981,852	869,456	25,116,341	25,920,998	-804,657	8,665,275
7	526,736,971	31,279,630	25,116,341	753,490	25,869,832	26,201,604	-331,772	8,333,503
8	531,695,262	31,604,218	25,869,832	776,095	26,645,927	26,460,806	185,121	8,518,624
9	536,151,674	31,901,716	26,645,927	799,378	27,445,304	26,696,173	749,131	9,267,755
10	540,052,111	32,169,100	27,445,304	823,359	28,268,663	26,905,095	1,363,569	10,631,324
11	548,654,176	32,403,127	28,268,663	848,060	23,801,061	27,217,657	-3,416,596	7,214,728
12	557,058,333	32,919,251	23,801,061	714,032	24,515,093	27,642,813	-3,127,720	4,087,009
13	565,231,287	33,423,500	24,515,093	735,453	25,250,546	28,057,241	-2,806,695	1,280,314
14	573,137,102	33,913,877	25,250,546	757,516	26,008,062	28,459,210	-2,451,147	-1,170,833
15	580,737,024	34,388,226	26,008,062	780,242	26,788,304	28,846,853	-2,058,549	-3,229,382
16	587,989,292	34,844,221	26,788,304	803,649	27,591,953	29,218,158	-1,626,205	-4,855,587
17	594,848,938	35,279,358	27,591,953	827,759	28,419,712	29,570,956	-1,151,244	-6,006,830
18	601,267,571	35,690,936	28,419,712	852,591	29,272,303	29,902,913	-630,609	-6,637,440
19	607,193,152	36,076,054	29,272,303	878,169	30,150,472	30,211,518	-61,046	-6,698,485
20	612,569,755	36,431,589	30,150,472	904,514	31,054,987	30,494,073	560,914	-6,137,571
21	617,337,304	36,754,185	31,054,987	931,650	31,986,636	30,747,676	1,238,960	-4,898,612
22	621,431,307	37,040,238	31,986,636	959,599	32,946,235	30,969,215	1,977,020	-2,921,592
23	624,782,563	37,285,878	32,946,235	988,387	33,934,622	31,155,347	2,779,276	-142,316
24	627,316,856	37,486,954	33,934,622	1,018,039	34,952,661	31,302,485	3,650,176	3,507,860
25	628,954,626	37,639,011	34,952,661	1,048,580	36,001,241	31,406,787	4,594,454	8,102,313

-5-
WHAT ARE YOU REALLY BUYING WHEN YOU <u>INVEST IN SECURITIES</u>

Anyone who purchases a stock must have some reason or rationale for doing so. Is it because they expect the stock to go up in price? Is it to diversify a portfolio? Is it to initiate a takeover? Is it to secure a stream of payments through dividends? Why did they choose that particular stock to purchase? Let's assume this someone is purchasing the stock for the most common of reasons, because they want to make money – they want a positive investment return. There are only two basic ways to make money when buying stock (and I emphasize "basic") – dividends and capital appreciation. There are more sophisticated (and risky) ways to make money, such as selling covered calls and securities lending. These other ways to monetize a holding of shares contain risks that go beyond just the stock going down in price.

The annuity stream provided by dividends is relatively easy to value using a discounted cash flow model. Though variables are involved, such as the volatility of the dividend stream in the future and the discount rate, I would venture to say that most investors feel comfortable putting a value on the dividend component. If you believe the dividends will be constant for the foreseeable future, then the portion of the stock price related to the dividend can be easily calculated.

That leaves the valuation of the capital appreciation component of the stock's price. There many different ways to calculate the portion representing capital appreciation – discounted cash flows, earnings growth, etc. If you believe that you are purchasing a portion of a company's future cash flows, then you can use a discounted cash flow model. If you believe that you are purchasing a share of the future earnings of the company, you can use an earnings based model. If you believe you are purchasing an interest in the growth of the company, you can use a model based on earnings growth. And, of course, you can combine models.

Economics would tell us that essentially the share price is a function of supply and demand – when there are more investors who want to buy the stock then there are sellers who will sell their shares, the price of the stock will rise. And the opposite holds as well – when there are more investors wishing to sell the stock then there are investors who are willing to purchase the stock, the price of the stock will go down.

What we know: We understand what we are buying when we invest in securities

The essence of this chapter is trying to determine what you are really buying when you purchase a share of stock. The underlying assumption is that if you believe you are buying stock and own a share of future cash flows, then the capital appreciation portion of the price you are willing to pay can be calculated using a discounted cash flow model. If you believe you are buying future earnings growth, then the capital appreciation portion can be described by a model using expected earnings growth. One's purpose in buying the stock weighs heavily on how they will evaluate it. If someone is purchasing an annuity, that is, a stream of regular payments expected to continue forever (dividends), then the discounted cash-flow model is appropriate. If they are purchasing the stock because they want to say that they own it, regardless of whether it will increase in value, then they are a collector and the only factor that matters is how good it will feel to tell people they are a shareholder. If they want to make money, that is, have a positive return from purchasing the stock, they have to ascertain what its value will be in the future.

I believe that what you are buying when you purchase a stock (with the intent of getting a positive return) is the hope that someone will pay you more for it in the future. Why would someone pay you more? Perhaps the general market has increased; perhaps the particular company has better results now then when you purchased it. Perhaps the prospective purchaser has no idea what they are doing and are making a huge mistake. It really doesn't matter which reason it is, as long as there is a buyer willing to pay more to purchase the share than you paid for it. I think all investors have seen a particular company's stock that has languished against similar company stock prices because somehow this company has not caught the public interest despite what looks like superior fundamentals – strong earnings, growth, market leadership, effective management, etc. Clearly the market can seem to be irrational at times.

Even an appropriate model relative to your goals is useful only if prospective purchasers use it. The model you utilize in determining whether the stock is a good investment is only relevant if a future purchaser uses the same model with the same assumptions. Because you are interested in an annuity stream, you may believe the stock price should be based on a discounted cash-flow model. If the population of future purchasers uses a different model to evaluate the stock, then there is no reason why what they consider a reasonable price to pay in purchasing the security is similar to what you consider a reasonable price to sell the security. Their model might indicate a higher value than your model, as well.

Models are seldom robust enough to be continually useful in explaining changes in stock price. Some have suggested that utilizing the price-earnings ratio (P-E) is helpful in stock picking. I am not so sure. Look at the P-E ratio of the S&P 500 from 1988 through 2011 (see Figure 19).

From 1988 through 2003, there seems to be a close parallel between the two graphs. Since then, however, there seems to be divergence. I am not willing to bet my money on a direct relationship between the P-E ratio and the index price after 2003. While the P-E ratio and the index value seemed highly correlated through 2003, that relationship does not continue since then.

Unless you invest in an index, you are not investing in the broad market but a much smaller subset. So, you won't be buying the whole S&P 500, but at best, some of the companies that are included in the index. This analysis makes sense when considering the index on the whole, but what we should really consider is particular stocks within the index. Could the P-E ratio of these selected stocks, if increasing relative to others, give them higher price appreciation and a better return? I think it is entirely possible, even likely. But. returning to an earlier point, only if a potential purchaser is using a P-E model to evaluate the price they are willing to pay.

Think of the stock market as a huge eBay where the only items available for sale are equity securities. Buyers and sellers come together and if they can agree on a price, consummate a transaction.

Figure 19
S&P 500 P-E Ratio

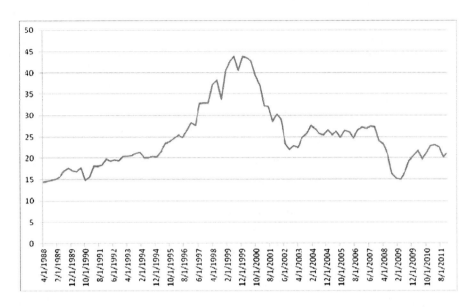

Now compare that to the graph of the index (see Figure 20).

Figure 20
S&P 500 Index

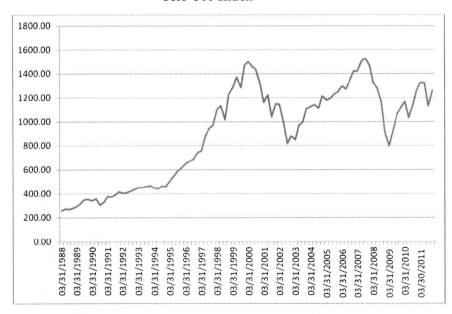

Now let's put them side-by-side (kind of) (Figure 21).

Figure 21
S&P 500 – Index value vs. P-E Ratio

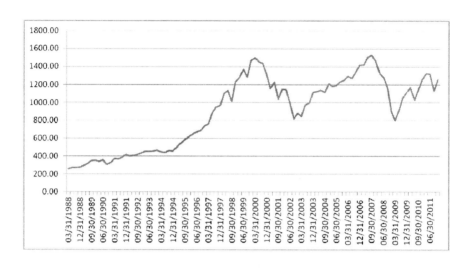

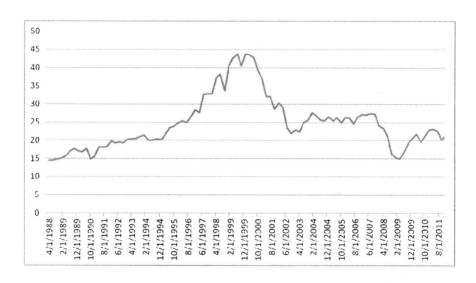

Let's get back to the eBay analogy. Say you own an art deco sterling silver beverage service, a beautiful set. You have the coffee pot, tea pot, cream pitcher, sugar bowl and five cups and saucers. There should be six cups and saucers, but something happened when you moved and the sixth set was lost. You happen to be on eBay and see the matching sixth cup and saucer. Assuming that having a complete set is meaningful to you, would you be more apt to bid higher than someone who just likes the design of the cup? Unless they have an unlimited amount of money and no regard for a good deal, the worth of that cup and saucer to you should be at the top of what anyone is willing to pay (assuming you are a collector with the same zeal with which I collect unnecessary artifacts).

There is no guarantee that the model you use in evaluating the worth of that cup and saucer is the same as another potential buyer. Maybe a potential buyer simply looks to purchase items where the silver content is worth more than current bid price. And what about how much the seller is willing to accept? Their lowest selling price might take into account silver content, pedigree, workmanship, condition and rarity. But if the item was a gift from a dear, departed loved one they might incorporate a valuation adjustment that makes the price all but prohibitive.

A flaw in this analogy is that the buyer with the incomplete tea service is not intending to sell the cup and saucer in the future, and therefore does not need to consider what someone else will pay, only what that cup and saucer is worth to them. The pertinent aspects of this analogy is that the seller of the cup and saucer, as well as other potential purchasers, are using different models to estimate the value and will come up with different prices. Someone buying stocks for the purpose of an investment has to be concerned with being able to recoup their cost and then some. I recognize this logical shortcoming, but hopefully the point of the analogy is made. There needs to a consistent basis used among buyers and sellers to evaluate the value of stocks, otherwise, it is just luck when you make money.

If you have ever watched a show on television where they do home improvements you will have heard them talk about "over-improving." This happens when the level of improvement is inappropriate for the house. The owner will enjoy the improvement, but won't see the cost of the improvement returned through increased market value. For instance, if you have a house that is valued at $150,000 (in a neighborhood of similarly priced homes) and you want to renovate the kitchen, an $80,000 renovation will increase the value of the house above $150,000, but it won't become $230,000. On the other hand, a

$15,000 kitchen renovation might make the house worth $165,000. The future value of the house in this case is highly dependent on external considerations. The model used to assess the future value of the renovated house will incorporate those limitations.

Sometimes valuation models are only relevant for a limited period (as we saw with the P-E ratio). During the dot-com era companies were evaluated (and valued) based on "eyeballs," the number of individuals who were attracted to their website. Companies were rewarded with high stock prices and enormous valuations. Of course you can't pay bills with people looking at your website; they need to be turned into participants in the revenue generating process. Eventually funders grew tired of investing money without a cohesive business plan or development of a reasonable exit strategy and the dot-com bubble burst. Clearly, future purchasers were not using the same valuation model as earlier purchasers of the shares.

-6-
<u>RISK</u>

Risk is a common term that is frequently used in an investment context. Firms have whole departments devoted to "risk management," and to be sure, potential investors want to kick the tires of the risk controls and procedures of firms under consideration. Defining and measuring risk is something investors expect of potential managers. Managers, for their part, have been diligent in providing qualitative and quantitative metrics regarding risk.

There are many types of risk that may be present – below is a partial list of different types of risk faced by managers and investors at an enterprise level[10]:

- Market risk	- Model risk	- Collateral risk
- Volatility risk	- Bankruptcy risk	- Headline risk
- Rollover risk	- Interest rate risk	- Correlation risk
- Reputation risk	- Legal risk	- Currency risk
- Regulatory risk	- Commodity risk	- Compliance risk
- Operational risk	- Personnel risk	- Counterparty risk
- Inflation risk	- Credit risk	- Country risk
- Terror risk	- Systemic risk	- Political risk
- Liquidity risk		

Fortunately, managers are fully cognizant of the various types of risks and more importantly, understand the procedures and protocols necessary to manage these risks. They provide risk reports to investors, and in meetings with investors leave no doubt that risk is a major concern and one that is

---

[10]The origin of my thoughts in this chapter stem from a paper I wrote "The Problems in Quantifying Risk," The *Journal of Applied Business and Economics*, Volume 12(2). I also need to credit Leslie Rahl for developing the first list of the different types of risk that I had seen.

professionally and competently managed. The tools at their disposal include VaR (value at risk), volatility calculations and the Sharpe ratio, to name a few. They also perform stress-testing to determine what would happen to the portfolio as variables move to extreme levels. Control parameters are set to avoid concentrations in items such as sector, geography, currency and other important factors. Reports are prepared to gauge where holdings fall relative to risk parameters. Systems are put in place to prevent unauthorized trades and to have investment committees approve all security purchases and sales. Policies are set regarding derivatives and leverage. Managers, consultants and investors have a good grip on risk.

What we know: Risk can be defined, identified, quantified and managed

The financial crisis is a recent and relevant example of the effectiveness of risk management. Managers thought they knew how much risk was in their portfolio. Investors and consultants thought they had a notion of how much risk they were willing to take, what their tolerance was and sought to include investments that met these parameters. All were wrong, the models failed, the pundits embarrassed themselves and the market dropped precipitously.

In order to manage risk, we first have to understand the definition of risk. Though it sounds simple, many do not have a working definition of risk. They are happy to throw the term around, but have trouble in defining it. If we want to talk about risk in terms that are known and agreed upon, we have to be in agreement about the definition of risk. Many times when I have met with a manager and they used the term "risk" I asked them to define the word. Most could not (a few could and gave what I would consider a very acceptable definition). To this end, I ask the following:

        - is "risk" a noun, verb or adjective?
        - is "risk" qualitative or quantitative?
        - is "risk" notional, relative or nominal?
        - is "risk" probabilistic, discrete, continuous or binary?
        - is "risk" normally distributed or follow some other distribution?

I think the answer to the questions above is "yes." And therein lays the problem. A single metric of risk can only be developed for those elements that are quantifiable on a similar scale and most investments embody multiple elements of a quantitative as well as a qualitative risk. Risk is a term that can be used in many contexts to describe many disparate situations. It can be used to describe the probability of a return not meeting a benchmark (return risk). At the same time, it can be used to describe the inability to remove cash from an investment (liquidity risk) where the investment has met the benchmark. And at the same time, it can be used to describe an investment that has met the benchmark and has the ability to provide cash redemptions but has failed to provide the non-correlation (correlation risk) that was expected.

Often there are investments that provide a multitude of crossover risk (think of investing with Bernie Madoff – you would have had return risk, liquidity risk, fraud risk, operational risk, headline risk, collateral risk, counterparty risk, systemic risk, reputation risk, legal risk and maybe some others). You may not have anticipated these risks, but they were there. The unfortunate problem with risk is that the complete list of all the risks involved in an investment is almost never accurately compiled until it is too late. Before Madoff admitted his transgressions, no investor in his fund would ever have thought that so many of the risk types applied to them. Understanding risk in retrospect is seldom helpful in relation to that investment.

Many investments carry a set of defined (but incomplete) risks from the outset. What has been interesting in this market environment is that new risks, previously unanticipated and unconsidered, have been appearing. There was the issue of securities lending where custodians and fund managers lent securities to enhance a return and wound up investing the collateral in securities that were subject to write-downs. That meant the return enhancement was not realized and the investor who provided the securities that were lent had to make up the reduction in the collateral, and the custodian and fund managers were forced to limit redemptions.

Not only were these risks not quantified, they were not even a consideration. Securities lending was previously thought to be a "no-brainer." Now investors often want agreements to specify that there will be no securities lending in any fund or account that they invest in. An index fund that had 1 day liquidity (meaning any or all of the investment can be withdrawn with 1 day notice) had the redemption provision changed so that investors may only remove 4% per month. Some hedge funds had redemption requests in excess of what they felt they could accommodate, despite the requests being in accord with the fund documents. So the hedge funds limited redemptions and transferred assets equal to the redemption requests to a liquidating trust fund. As the trust fund sells assets, cash will be distributed. What should have happened in 5 days (most hedge funds allow an annual withdrawal, often on December 31 with around 45 days notice) will now take the better part of 12 – 24 months to accomplish, with the investors responsible for the additional costs of the trust fund.

The holy grail of risk measurement would be a single measure that nicely encapsulates all risks an enterprise might face. And there are those firms that will sell you this single measure. The problem is that some risks are qualitative, some quantitative – how do you establish a single numeric that handles both? Risks might be distributed based on differing curves, depending on the risk – how do you normalize? Some risks might be binary or continuous or discrete – how do you assemble into a single figure?

It would appear that a single measure of risk not only is not achievable, but not be might useful. The purpose of measuring risk is to allow an investor to structure a portfolio to meet predetermined criteria, such as perpetuity and the target return contained in the investment policy statement. The financial world has had a rough awakening to the idea that despite the appearance of having useful quantitative analysis around risk, they had no idea what they were talking about, used flawed models, and worse, cannot agree on a definition of risk. Stress-testing can be an excellent tool, provided that all relevant variables are identified and included in the model. The history of financial crises is that the crisis is caused by elements that were previously not contemplated and hence, left out of the model.

In any portfolio that is subject to stress-testing the limitation on the usefulness is the missing variables. The variables are missing because they have not been thought of. This omission requires every model to contain a "noise" component. To some, the noise component represents the normal random variations that may occur. To me, the noise component represents the important, unidentified missing variables that should have been in the model but weren't. How much weight should this noise factor have on the model is a matter of opinion. The more robust and complete the model, the less weight the noise component should carry. The problem is that we never know how complete or robust the model is until it stops working. I would suggest a noise component that carries an adjustment factor of 50 – 80% is probably right. That level of adjustment would be extremely unpopular, but possibly necessary.

In the end, the question becomes where investors go from here. Should they stop considering risk? Should they limit the discussion of risk to those items that they can understand and analyze? It is not an easy answer. There would seem to be little benefit in discussing the elements of risk that are known, defined and quantified when these items do not represent the true danger to an investment. Yet to ignore them seems foolhardy. And you can't discuss things you haven't identified. The best we can do is to understand the limitations inherent in discussions of risk and realize that the potential downside is contained in uncharted waters.

-7-
<u>BENCHMARKS</u>

Benchmarks occupy a prominent place in portfolio evaluation and usually form the basis for assessing manager performance. Benchmarks are employed at an investment level to answer the question, "Did I choose the right manager?" and in assessing whether the manager delivered "alpha" – a return above the benchmark. Generally, the benchmark represents a low-cost investment alternative (such as an index) that invests within the same investment strategy as the manager it is applied to. This seems to be a very reasonable approach, since fiduciaries of a portfolio engaged in hiring managers need to be able to evaluate their choices. Comparing the returns of the manager chosen against a related index seems to be highly appropriate.

If no benchmark was chosen, manager performance would be hard to assess. Let's say you hired a manager to invest in stocks that were part of the S&P 500. For a given year that manager delivered a 4% return (net of fees). Was this satisfactory performance? Well, if the S&P 500 index had a return of -10% for that same period, evaluation of the manager would indicate one thing, whereas if the S&P 500 returned 20% for that same period, the evaluation might indicate something else entirely. A singular return figure would be hard to assess without something to compare it to. For manager evaluation, that something is usually a benchmark.

Sometimes a manager has an investment mandate that is broader than what a single index can capture, so benchmarks are frequently a blend of various indices. Sometimes a static adjustment is added to a benchmark (such as 30 day US Treasury Bills plus 5%). Any benchmark should be investable and relevant to the investment mandate the manager has. Likewise, static adjustments should not be arbitrary, but based on what the manager is expected to, and agrees to, deliver.

Just as the fiduciaries of a portfolio need to be able to evaluate the performance of the managers they hire, the fiduciaries should be evaluated as well. Portfolio evaluation also usually employs a benchmark and often more than a single benchmark. A typical institutional portfolio may have a blend of equity and debt benchmarks, perhaps along the line of using a blend of 70% equity and 30% debt (similar to the asset allocation scheme the organization employs). With the prevalence of international investing, using a global equity index and a broad global debt index could better parallel the asset allocation of the portfolio.

What we know: The use of an appropriate benchmark is a useful tool

The widespread use of benchmarks has caused numerous long-term problems in investing. Managers are aware of the benchmark against which they are evaluated and know the components of the benchmark – which stocks or bonds are included and the weighting each has. For any given strategy, the individual securities chosen by the fund manager is bound to contain some overlap with the index – after all, an appropriate index will incorporate a sample (or the entirety) of the investable population from which the manager is selecting investments.

This has led to the establishment of a metric called "active share[11]." This metric looks (and I am paraphrasing the essence of it) at the components of the benchmark and similar securities held by the fund manager and provides the deviations between the relative proportions. Let's say a manager held a stock and it comprised 5% of his portfolio. If the benchmark index also included that security and it comprised 5% of the index, then the manager did nothing with respect to that stock except replicate the index. Why pay a management fee for that?

Benchmarks put an onus on a manager to outperform the index. By staying within a strategy and not straying, the manager needs to overweight the securities that will perform better and underweight (or avoid all-together) the securities that will perform worse. As simple as this may sound, in many markets it is very difficult to continually outperform a benchmark. This inevitably leads to numerous, somewhat undesirable conclusions, such as

---

[11]Cremers, Martijn and Petajisto, Antti, How Active is Your Fund Manager? A New Measure That Predicts Performance (March 31, 2009). AFA 2007 Chicago Meetings Paper; EFA 2007 Ljubljana Meetings Paper; Yale ICF Working Paper No. 06-14. Available at SSRN: http://ssrn.com/abstract=891719

avoiding a strategy, choosing a passive investment, such as an index (which may not be a bad thing, except from the perspective of the managers and the fiduciaries managing the portfolio – their importance becomes greatly diminished) or constantly changing managers (once the manager outperforms or underperforms the benchmark for a couple of periods it is time to move on to another manager).

And despite these shortcomings, the biggest problem with benchmarks is that they do not answer the question they are designed to answer. If the question is "was the manager choice the correct one," then the benchmark does not provide the answer. The answer is provided by a comparison to what the alternative choice of investment was. Most institutional investors I know are looking at multiple managers for investment in a given strategy. If they decide to go with Manager A, then the alternative is usually not an index, but Manager B. The true comparison should be between Manager A and B – would they have been better off, over some chosen time horizon, going with Manager B?

Evaluations of manager performance tend to treat the benchmark as the alternative investment choice, when most investors would not select an index had they not chosen the manager they did. They would choose a different manager. Yet this is seldom part of the evaluative criteria.

Another problem arises when benchmarking the overall portfolio. A typical institutional investment policy statement will include multiple goals, such as perpetuity and a target return of a "real X%." Let's say the X represents something between 5 and 6 percent. For discussion, let's use 5% as the target return (comprising both the real portion and the X% portion). Portfolios are seldom evaluated against the real 5%. The portfolio is evaluated against the benchmark, blended or otherwise, often in quartile terms against peer groups.

If the fiduciary for a given portfolio delivered that real 5% return every year, they should be well-regarded – they delivered the performance they were hired to. Would they be rewarded for continuously delivering the target? Probably not. Comparison of the performance of the portfolio against the benchmark might lead to a different conclusion about how well they performed. And comparison to peer quartiles might add additional evidence that the portfolio (and the fiduciaries) underperformed.

For institutional investors who have a target return of 8% (combining spending of 5.5% and inflation of 2.5%), how many would go back in time, knowing what they know today, and invest in US Government Bonds and lock up the 8% return for the foreseeable future? Probably not many, though it can be argued that that is exactly what they should do. Of course, if during the next ten years inflation ran at 10%, it may not look like such a good idea.

Benchmarks can be useful as one metric among many in evaluating mangers and portfolios. But when benchmarks are the center (or only) element in an evaluation, there is a tendency to treat the benchmark as something it is not – an alternative investment strategy. If the entity would consider an index as a potential investment, then the index should be included in the short list of managers competing for a mandate within a given strategy. But if the entity would not allocate to an index, then the subset of the population of investable choices should be comprised of the potential manager selections, and the performance of the managers not selected should represent the benchmark.

For the portfolio taken as a whole, the evaluation of the performance of the fiduciaries should be conducted along the lines of their directive as contained in the investment policy statement. Did they do what they were hired to do? If so, then benchmarks and peer comparisons are secondary and tertiary, not primary, information.

-8-
FEES

Would you invest in a fund that charged a 2% management fee and a 20% performance fee? Among institutional investors the answer probably is "I already do." Commonly referred to as "2 and 20" this is a common fee structure for hedge funds and similar vehicles. Different investment structures tend to have different fee arrangements and fees can also vary somewhat from manager to manager. Retail investors have long believed that selecting a mutual fund starts with looking at fee structures. Vanguard has built a business on offering funds with low fees.

The net returns of two funds that bought the exact same securities at the same time, at the same price, and sold them at the same time and at the same price, would be differentiated by fees. The one with the lower fees would provide the higher return net of fees (assuming their expenses were the same as well, something usually overlooked in fee discussions). But how often do two funds buy the exact same securities at the same time at the same price?

Fees deserve careful consideration. When thinking of making an investment there are reams of past history. But what an investor cares about is how the investment will perform tomorrow, not yesterday. To this end, the only concrete information available related to the future are the fees. The fees are contractually limited and defined. The performance of the fund in the future is not predictable, but the fees are. While not being the only consideration, among managers that are considered equivalent, why not choose the one with the lower fees?

What we know: Fees are an important consideration in manager selection

The fees act as an initial hurdle. Take two funds, where one fund is charging 50 basis points and the fee of the other fund is 100 basis points. The second fund has to return 50 more basis points than the first just to offset the higher fee. This differential is especially telling at lower returns. At higher fund returns the fee differential becomes less important. Figure 22 below takes two funds, one charging a fee of 50 basis points and the other a fee of 100 points and shows the fee differential at varying gross returns.

Given the same gross returns, the lower fee option will always be 50 basis points better. But why assume that the gross returns will be the same? If there is value in the higher fee, such as a better track record, maybe the fund with the higher fees are a better investment. Where the rubber meets the road with investing is the return after deducting fees and expenses (the net return). Similarly, there is no reason to assume that a higher fee brings more value. Maybe the higher fee is based on reputation rather than performance. An investor is simply a consumer when shopping for a manager, and as consumers should recognize, there will be good deals and there will be bad deals. Unlike the purchase of durable goods where we can be reasonably assured that the reviews of the product we are considering will relate to the future as well as the past, with investments we can only be reasonably assured of the past.

Imagine trying to buy a household appliance. The appliance has been on the market for quite some time and has been reviewed and tested numerous times by many reputable third parties, as well as previous purchasers. One might feel well-informed about the potential to be pleased with this purchase. Now suppose that the product you are considering comes with this disclaimer: "The product looks the same as the products sold in the past; however, the product may have been produced by a different factory employing different materials and subjected to different quality control tests. There is no way to tell whether the product will perform as in the past."

Isn't this essentially the disclaimer on financial products? The product looks the same – meaning the product has the same name and same strategy. The product may have been produced by a different factory – meaning that personnel may have changed, the portfolio manager and analyst team may be different. The product may employ different materials – meaning that style drift may occur within the boundaries of the investment mandate. The product is subject to different quality controls – the risk management controls may not be updated for changing market scenarios or may not incorporate previously unconsidered or unidentified risks. There is no way to tell whether the product will perform as in the past – which translates to past performance is no guarantee of future performance.

Figure 22
Return Differential Based on Fees

Gross Return	Fees A	Fees B	Return, Net A	Return, Net B	% A Over B
1.0%	0.5%	1.0%	0.5%	0.0%	N/A
2.0%	0.5%	1.0%	1.5%	1.0%	50.0%
3.0%	0.5%	1.0%	2.5%	2.0%	25.0%
4.0%	0.5%	1.0%	3.5%	3.0%	16.7%
5.0%	0.5%	1.0%	4.5%	4.0%	12.5%
6.0%	0.5%	1.0%	5.5%	5.0%	10.0%
7.0%	0.5%	1.0%	6.5%	6.0%	8.3%
8.0%	0.5%	1.0%	7.5%	7.0%	7.1%
9.0%	0.5%	1.0%	8.5%	8.0%	6.2%
10.0%	0.5%	1.0%	9.5%	9.0%	5.6%
11.0%	0.5%	1.0%	10.5%	10.0%	5.0%
12.0%	0.5%	1.0%	11.5%	11.0%	4.5%
13.0%	0.5%	1.0%	12.5%	12.0%	4.2%
14.0%	0.5%	1.0%	13.5%	13.0%	3.8%
15.0%	0.5%	1.0%	14.5%	14.0%	3.6%
16.0%	0.5%	1.0%	15.5%	15.0%	3.3%
17.0%	0.5%	1.0%	16.5%	16.0%	3.1%
18.0%	0.5%	1.0%	17.5%	17.0%	2.9%
19.0%	0.5%	1.0%	18.5%	18.0%	2.8%
20.0%	0.5%	1.0%	19.5%	19.0%	2.6%

The key question is not which fee is less, but what a higher fee provides. If the investor decides there is value in the higher fee, then it may not be a critical detriment. Years ago there was a saying I heard that seems to bear importance: "Cost is only relevant in the absence of value."[12] That higher fee may or may not be warranted, but just ruling out an investment because of a higher fee may be counterproductive.

Perhaps the best way I can think of to encapsulate my thoughts about fees, is to say that the manager you did not like who had a 65 basis point fee will not be

---

[12] I do not know who originated the quote, but I heard it from Charles Parisi, my former college roommate and good friend.

any more liked at a fee of 50 basis points and one that you have been thrilled with at 75 basis points will still be liked at a fee of 85 basis points.

-9-
<u>OUTSOURCING</u>

Outsourcing comes in many forms and exists in varying degrees and covers a broad spectrum of connotation. To many, outsourcing represents turning over the portfolio to a third party to make all decisions, including asset allocation, manager selection and risk tolerance. To organizations that have historically self-managed their portfolio, this ceding of control is uncomfortable and unacceptable.

There are numerous stories about rogue traders working for financial services firms who have bankrupted the firm they worked for by making unauthorized trades. The worry of every fiduciary in giving up control is to put the institution out of business by allowing an outsider to have unchecked control over the portfolio investments.

No one can understand the organization, its needs and its goals, with the depth and breadth the extent that the employees and trustees can. These are the individuals who work on a daily basis to make the organization a success. These people do not have split allegiances, do not have to balance the needs of other clients and factions and do not worry about performance bonuses[13]. Their only concern is the good of the entity and the fulfillment of the investment goals to enable the organization to pursue its mission.

Outsiders, whose mission statement and corporate goals may be very different from its clients, cannot possess the same level of loyalty and fealty that staff and trustees bring to the organization. The goals of these outsiders are for the good of their company and the betterment of their staff. When these coincide with the goals of their clients it is a wonderful thing. But when they conflict, whose

---

[13]I recognize that many internal investment staffs are incentivized and do care about bonuses. The paragraph just reads so much better ignoring that fact.

goals would be paramount? During the financial crisis there were many organizations who requested redemptions from their managers. The actions of some of the managers left the clients wondering whose interests the managers were serving – the remaining clients or their own. It was apparent to everyone that most managers did not have the interests of the redeeming clients as a priority. It seems that too often the interests of the managers outweighed the interests of the clients. On a fully outsourced basis this potential fear increases at a geometric rate.

Some investments utilize a black-box model – there is no transparency about how investment decisions are made. The investor has to trust that the manager knows what they are doing, has the proper controls in place and follows this undisclosed model. Outsourcing can be analogous. The loss of control often leads investors to alternative ways to access given markets. An old adage in investing is never to invest in something you don't understand. With a black-box model you cannot understand it because you are never told how it works. With black-box investing the most you can lose is the investment. You can minimize the maximum harm to the portfolio by investing only a small portion of the total. With outsourcing the portfolio, the most you can lose is everything.

What we know: Outsourcing the management of a portfolio is a marked change in structure

Some investors have a well-developed and fully staffed investment office. With this level of infrastructure and expertise they make individual security selections. This chapter does not apply to them. Outsourcing would be a marked change in their structure and approach. At the extreme, they may use no discernible outsourcing – no consultants, no managers. But the group of institutional investors that fall into this category is incredibly small. For the remaining entities, which represent the vast majority of organizations, they probably are already engaged in outsourcing. The only question is to what extent. Many investors utilize the services of a consultant. The consultant may perform due diligence on prospective managers, may recommend asset allocation changes and may prepare performance analytics. This is a low level of outsourcing, but outsourcing nonetheless. Consultants may have access to managers that institutions, on their own, would be unable to invest in. Consultants provide intellectual capital and connections that investors may lack. The overwhelming majority of investors do not select securities, they select managers. The managers select the securities. This represents another level of outsourcing. Figure 23 provides us with a visual example with the hierarchy of outsourcing.

Figure 23
Outsourcing Hierarchy

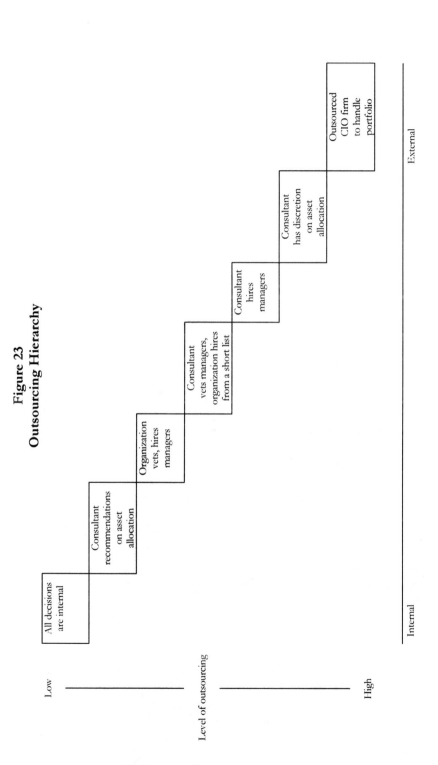

Depending where your organization falls on Figure 23 will determine how big a leap it is to fully outsource the entire portfolio. For organizations that fall to the very left of the chart, outsourcing the entire portfolio represents an incomprehensible leap. The further to the right your organization is, the less of a leap outsourcing the entire portfolio turns out to be.

A typical institutional investor structure has the organization responsible for asset allocation and perhaps the final say on manager hires. A consultant will make recommendations as to asset allocation, the acceptance and implementation falling to the investment committee (or other decision-making body) of the entity. Any organization can decide when they should radically diverge from the consultant's recommendation. Being able to disagree and go a different route may be an important element of how the portfolio is managed, but if this seldom (or never) happens, how important is it to keep this control? I am not suggesting that institutional investors rubber-stamp their consultant's recommendations. What I would suggest is that an organization that constantly finds itself disagreeing with the consultant will most likely find another consultant.

Consultants often perform due diligence on potential managers and deliver a short list of managers when necessary. The organization makes the final decision. How often does the selection not come from the short list? The organization has essentially outsourced a major element of manager selection – developing the short list. This is no knock on consultants – they perform essential services and allow organizations to have effective and efficient investment offices with low overhead. But we should acknowledge that consultants are the first level of outsourcing.

If we define outsourcing as the level to which one allows a third party discretion, then we have to carefully consider what discretion means. Clearly making a final decision on a particular question would be discretion. But wouldn't providing a short list be considered discretion as well? An extreme example would be the first buyers of Model-T Fords, who had discretion over the color of the vehicle. They could select any color from the palette available. Unfortunately, the only color available was black. Suppose a Model-T buyer could choose between two colors – they would have discretion in color choice, but only from the limited availability provided by the manufacturer. This short listing of color choice significantly limits a purchaser's options, though the purchaser still has their choice of color.

Anytime a third party is allowed to pare choices down to a small subset, they have exercised considerable discretion. Investors tend to only think in terms of the final decision as being discretion, but any limitations imposed on the choices presented represents some level of discretion.

Continuing this thought, an investor looking at the level of discretion awarded to a third party might be surprised to see that they are delegating more of the decision-making than they originally thought. Investors know that they have delegated security selection to managers, but if they accurately assess the total level of discretion, they might conclude that fully outsourcing the management of the portfolio is not so great a leap. After careful reflection they might come to the conclusion that the only decision-making elements they currently retain for themselves are asset allocation and manager selection, and these are largely entrusted to the recommendations of a consultant.

-10-
ALTERNATIVE ASSETS

In the late 1970s and early 1980s, university endowments started investing in an asset class labeled "alternative assets." Shortly thereafter, foundations started investing in alternative assets along with family offices, sovereign wealth funds and to a much lesser extent, pension plans. Today, it is not surprising to see that endowments can be 50% invested in alternatives, and foundations in the 30% range. When we talk about alternative assets we usually include hedge funds, private equity, venture capital, natural resources, timber, oil and gas and real estate. These investment vehicles usually possess little or no transparency, often a limited partnership structure (though certainly not exclusively), model-based valuations and extended time frames from initial investment to final distribution. It would not be unusual for alternative asset managers to utilize derivatives in their portfolio, but it is not a requirement for inclusion on the list of alternative assets. In a sense, the term "alternative" means an investment structure that is an alternative to what was the typical investment structure – long-only managers using a commingled fund (mutual fund) structure or providing a separate account.

Alternative assets can be marketable (commonly called MALT, for marketable alternative assets) or non-MALT (for non-marketable alternative assets). Hedge funds are usually included as marketable alternative assets, while the list of non-marketable alternative assets would contain investments such as private equity, venture capital, oil and gas, energy, natural resources, timber and other types of structures that did not allow redemptions but returned investor money though distributions over extended time periods.

The term "marketable" relates to the holdings of the investment fund, and whether there was a ready market for the investments they hold. The term does not imply that investors in these funds have a commensurate level of liquidity.

An alternative asset fund that held fully marketable securities (those traded on a major exchange) might have redemption requirements that limit investors to request redemptions once per year with a specified amount of notice.

What we know: We can define what an alternative asset is

Interestingly enough, what constitutes an alternative asset is hard to define. Alternative assets are usually described by a list of those investments that are included as alternatives (hedge funds, private equity, venture capital, real estate, timber, natural resources, oil and gas, to name a few). But what makes these alternative assets? A definition of a term should not be described by a list of what is usually included when talking about that term – there should be a narrative way to define what is considered an alternative asset (and/or what isn't). You can invest in real estate through a REIT (real estate investment trust), which is publicly traded. Why should a limited partnership (the usual vehicle for a real estate alternative asset) be considered an alternative asset? What are the inherent characteristics that make it alternative? The REIT, by virtue of being a security traded on an exchange and subject to filing and reporting requirements, might have a lot more transparency than a real estate limited partnership. But transparency has come a long way and it is not hard to find examples in every sector of investing where there is an "alternative" with extensive transparency.

Having an asset class comprised of alternative assets does not accomplish much, since the holdings of alternative asset funds might overlap the holdings of traditional managers. Unless the investor looks through the holdings, meaning they parse the holdings of the alternative asset funds and reclassify the individual investments held to the asset classes they use to manage their portfolio, they will not get a true sense of whether any concentrations exist and whether the actual asset allocation is in accord with their model portfolio. In a real sense there may not exist a standard definition of what an alternative asset is. And it may not be important to offer a definition for "alternative assets" since it really does not help manage the portfolio. I believe that the holdings in anything categorized as an alternative asset have to be reclassified based on every cut of the portfolio that is done (asset allocation, risk, liquidity, sector, geography, currency, etc.). There is virtually no way to slice a portfolio when having an allocation to alternative assets. Without this reclassification when looking at asset allocation, risk, liquidity, sectors, geography, currency, etc., the holdings of the alternative investments need to be reclassified to the relevant category. All alternative asset funds have holdings that span across multiple categories and elude effective categorization.

-11-
ALTERNATIVE ASSET RETURNS

I was at a conference in New York City in early 2009 and a panelist asked the audience a question – "What was the business of an alternative asset fund?" He answered his question by saying – "Raising the next fund." The cynical nature of his commentary is not unusual when it comes to alternative asset funds. Alternative asset funds often market a new fund during the lifetime of their other funds which are running under the stewardship of common management. The marketing materials of the new fund would include the interim results of the existing funds, which are largely self-reported.

It would seem that funds currently marketing new funds would have an incentive to overstate the interim rates of return. These interim rates of return are based on the market value of the assets held in the fund. Calculating the market value of the holdings can be a tricky art and seldom is it science. Overstating the value of the holdings will overstate the reported internal rates of return. These returns are unrealized, meaning that the return is not supported by transactions resulting from an arms-length sale. They are paper or holding gains. Returns to the investors are only realized through cash distributions. If a manager did overstate the value of the holdings and therefore overstated the internal rates of return (whether intentionally or not), the cash flows back to the investors would not support the reported interim rates of return. In the end, the unrealized gains in the alternative asset fund would never become realized.

Given the ability to overstate returns and the apparent benefit from doing so, it would not be surprising that managers would tend to use market values at the upper end of any reasonable range. There is even no need to ascribe ill will to the managers – it could very well be that individuals tend to think of their property as worth more than it actually is. Anyone who has ever tried to buy a house has probably encountered more sellers who thought their house was worth more than the market thought as opposed to the opposite situation.

What we know: Alternative asset returns tend to be overstated as a result of valuations based on manager estimates

Alternative asset funds are usually formed using a limited partnership structure and generally have limited lives (ten years is common), which can be extended depending on market conditions and the progress of winding-up the residual holdings. As a group, alternative assets consist of private equity, venture capital, real estate, natural resources, oil and gas, timber, infrastructure and hedge funds. I purposely omit hedge funds from the group because a characteristic of the hedge fund structure is that it usually does not possess a limited life. For the purposes of this chapter a limited life is an important characteristic.

During the life of an alternative asset fund, returns are reported by the fund manager. These returns are "unrealized." Realized returns are based strictly upon cash distributions, which can occur during the entire life of the fund, but more commonly occur during the middle and end of the fund's life span. The flow of an alternative asset fund's life is[14]:

1. Fund is set up (legal organization)
2. Fund is launched (announced as "open")
3. Solicitation of interest and commitment (capital raising)
4. Fund "closes" (actual start)
5. Investments are identified and capital is called
6. Distributions are made to investors (sometimes during the period while capital is still being called)
7. Fund is wound down (all holdings liquidated and final distribution to investors is made)

The initial and middle period of the fund's life (after the fund closes) is spent acquiring assets, re-positioning and improving these assets and making management changes. The final stage of a fund's life is the sale of the improved holdings and return of capital (distributions) to the investors. It should be noted that sometimes dispositions happen very early in the process (for example, the Blackstone purchase of Equity Office Properties saw Blackstone

---

[14]Much of this section comes from a paper I wrote with Andy Braunstein and George Mangiero: "Do the unrealized gains in alternative investments ever become realized?" *Journal of Investing*, Vol. 19, No. 2, Summer 2010, pp 49-52.

engage in a large number of sales transactions almost simultaneously with the purchase).

When all is said and done, the actual (true) return of the alternative asset fund is the rate of return that results when putting cash contributions (calls) and distributions on a time line. By taking a sample of funds with a vintage of around 2000 (year of origin) and that have finished distributing to the owners and have liquidated, and looking at the reported unrealized gains throughout the fund's life, a comparison can be made of the actual rate of return (based on the timeline of calls and distributions) and the reported rate of return. The information that was available for the sample of funds is contributions, distributions, and reported rates of return. Utilizing this data allows an informal evaluation (due to the small sample size) of the accuracy of the reported interim internal rate of return for funds of this sort.

In the end, the only true determination of how the fund actually performed is to conduct a comparison of the cash flows provided by the investors to the fund (the "calls") against the cash flows provided by the fund back to the investors (the "distributions"). Alternative assets have a fairly long life (usually ten years as a minimum and often the life is extended to get more favorable terms on disposition of remaining holdings) and during the middle of the life cycle there is often a mixing of capital inflows from investors to the fund at the same time that the fund is making distributions back to the investors.

If it is true that alternative asset managers have an incentive to overstate interim returns if they are raising another fund, the converse may be true as well – funds not raising another fund do not have an incentive to overstate returns and therefore their reported and true returns will tend to be closer.

The internal rate of return (IRR) is defined as the discount rate that makes the present value of all the cash flows (inflows and outflows) equal to exactly $0.00. We used 14 alternative asset funds (a small sample to be sure) that had wound down and finished making distributions to the investors.

Figure 24 below displays the results for the preliminary sample of fourteen alternative asset funds. For all fourteen of the funds listed, the entire original commitment was actually contributed over time, and, after a series of distributions, the life of the fund was determined to have come to an end. The stated return was the interim rates of return provided by the manager to the investor during the life of the fund. The calculated return was the actual or true return derived by looking at the timing and amount of the cash flows.

93

Figure 24
Summary of Results

| Fund | Average Annual: | | Raising |
	Stated Return	Calculated Return	New Funds?
1	22.99	22.99	N
2	48.80	45.67	Y
3	7.92	3.48	N
4	13.19	15.66	Y
5	12.71	20.77	Y
6	33.55	34.45	Y
7	18.13	24.25	Y
8	12.40	19.51	N
9	23.21	22.82	N
10	49.59	47.55	Y
11	76.20	68.91	N
12	10.47	11.93	Y
13	71.79	62.19	Y
14	8.93	11.03	N

The value in the "stated return" column represents the arithmetic mean of the annual returns as reported by the fund manager. These are the unrealized returns. The value in the "calculated return" column represents the calculated internal rate of return of the actual cash flows (contributions and distributions) for the fund. These are the realized or "true" returns.

From Figure 24 we see that eight of the fourteen funds that were included in the sample were raising capital for a new fund during the operation of the current fund. We hypothesized that, for those funds, marketing strategy might lead to a situation where the stated return exceeded the calculated return. Likewise, for funds not currently marketing new ones, we expected that the stated return was not as likely to exceed the calculated return. From this small sample, the results appear to be mixed in terms of whether there is a difference between funds that were raising a new fund, and those that were not. Of those funds marketing new funds, only three out of the eight have calculated returns overstating the actual returns. For funds not currently marketing new ones, three out of the six have reported returns overstating the actual returns (although it is by less than one half of one percent in one of those cases).

Of course, when we say that of the eight that were raising new funds three were found to overstate the returns, we are also saying that five did not overstate the returns. Some of the reported returns were overstated (two substantially, depending on what you would consider a substantial overstatement), and some understated – there was one fund where the reported returns and actual returns were the same, 6 funds where the reported returns overstated the actual returns and 7 funds where the reported returns understated the returns. Given that it was a small sample and some mixed results, it still appeared to us that alternative asset managers were reporting rates of return more often conservatively rather than aggressively.

After we began thinking about these results, we were curious about the sensitivity of the results – would a small change in any variable cause a change in the evaluation of the reported return versus the actual return, or were the results robust?

We chose one of the 14 funds (Fund 3) that was deemed a fund that over-reported the true rate of return and put the cash contributions and distributions on a time line[15]. In the case of this fund, they drew all the cash first and then later came the distributions. There was no overlap. The amount of the contributions and distributions are shown in Figure 25.

---

[15]The bulk of this section comes from a paper I wrote with Andy Braunstein, "The Accuracy of the Rates of Return Reported By Fund Managers: A Test in the United States," *International Journal of Management*, Volume 28, Number 1, Part 1, March 2011.

Figure 25
Fund Cash Flows

Contribution	Distribution
20,000	0
60,000	0
0	0
60,000	0
40,000	0
80,000	0
81,000	0
0	0
80,000	0
160,000	0
139,000	0
40,000	0
80,000	0
160,000	0
70,000	0
135,000	0
80,000	0
190,000	0
164,000	0
0	0
0	0
41,000	0
99,900	0
40,100	0
0	0
0	0
180,000	0
0	0
0	2,305,735
0	42,900
0	92,193

0	715,745
0	292,563
0	0
0	0
0	0
0	0
0	0
0	0
0	0
0	0
0	0
0	0
0	0
0	0
0	0
0	0
0	0
0	0
0	0
0	0
0	0
0	37,000
0	775
2,000,000	3,486,911

One can see that, overall, the fund returned more than was contributed. Recall from Figure 24 that the "true" rate of return was calculated as 3.48%, versus a reported return of 7.92%, leading us to conclude that the fund's returns were over-reported. The next step was to adjust the cash flows by the reported quarterly returns to get a cumulative balance, incorporating contributions, distributions and returns. This is done in Figure 26.

Figure 26
Cash Flows Adjusted By Reported Quarterly Returns

Contribution	Distribution	Net Cash Flow	IRR	Balance with IRR
20,000	0	20,000	0.00%	20,000
60,000	0	80,000	-7.19%	78,562
0	0	80,000	-5.17%	77,547
60,000	0	140,000	-64.56%	115,347
40,000	0	180,000	-48.00%	136,705
80,000	0	260,000	-8.02%	212,360
81,000	0	341,000	-5.78%	289,121
0	0	341,000	2.03%	290,588
80,000	0	421,000	0.00%	370,588
160,000	0	581,000	0.00%	530,588
139,000	0	720,000	0.00%	669,588
40,000	0	760,000	0.00%	709,588
80,000	0	840,000	0.00%	789,588
160,000	0	1,000,000	2.91%	956,497
70,000	0	1,070,000	2.43%	1,032,733
135,000	0	1,205,000	16.40%	1,215,610
80,000	0	1,285,000	14.11%	1,341,312
190,000	0	1,475,000	12.24%	1,578,170
164,000	0	1,639,000	10.64%	1,788,512
0	0	1,639,000	7.02%	1,819,900
0	0	1,639,000	6.27%	1,848,427
41,000	0	1,680,000	-6.00%	1,861,086
99,900	0	1,779,900	-5.78%	1,932,650
40,100	0	1,820,000	-3.27%	1,956,622
0	0	1,820,000	-2.91%	1,942,388
0	0	1,820,000	0.37%	1,944,185
180,000	0	2,000,000	0.19%	2,125,194
0	0	2,000,000	14.69%	2,203,241
0	2,305,735	-305,735	14.41%	-106,186
0	42,900	-348,635	15.47%	-154,852
0	92,193	-440,828	15.07%	-256,352
0	715,745	-1,156,573	18.11%	-1,016,109
0	292,563	-1,449,136	17.72%	-1,366,646
0	0	-1,449,136	17.34%	-1,425,890
0	0	-1,449,136	17.18%	-1,487,132
0	0	-1,449,136	16.67%	-1,549,108
0	0	-1,449,136	16.54%	-1,613,164
0	0	-1,449,136	16.08%	-1,678,013

0	0	-1,449,136	15.97%	-1,745,008
0	0	-1,449,136	15.88%	-1,814,285
0	0	-1,449,136	15.81%	-1,885,994
0	0	-1,449,136	15.69%	-1,959,972
0	0	-1,449,136	15.63%	-2,036,558
0	0	-1,449,136	15.05%	-2,113,184
0	0	-1,449,136	15.01%	-2,192,481
0	0	-1,449,136	14.98%	-2,274,589
0	0	-1,449,136	14.94%	-2,359,545
0	0	-1,449,136	14.91%	-2,447,497
0	0	-1,449,136	14.90%	-2,538,667
0	0	-1,449,136	14.89%	-2,633,169
0	0	-1,449,136	14.87%	-2,731,057
0	0	-1,449,136	14.86%	-2,832,515
0	37,000	-1,486,136	14.66%	-2,974,683
0	775	-1,486,911	14.66%	-3,084,509

It is easy to see that the fund actually under-reported the returns. At the point the first distribution was made, the fund should have had $2,203,241 available to distribute (the balance of all contributions plus the quarterly reported returns). Not only did the fund distribute more than this, but the fund had excess holdings to the extent that future distributions could be made.

We then set about analyzing the actual extent to which this particular fund had under-reported the returns. We applied a static adjustment to each quarterly reported return. In the case of Fund 3, we found (using trial and error) that we had to add 10.70% to each quarterly return in order for the balance after the last distribution to be zero (0).

We applied the same methodology to the remaining 13 funds. The necessary static adjustments (to two decimal places) for the entire set of funds are shown as Figure 27.

Note that each of the 14 funds in the sample has a positive static adjustment. This leads to the inference that the reported returns were less than the actual returns in the case of all fourteen funds. We sort the static adjustments in descending order in Figure 28.

Figure 27
Static Adjustments

Fund	Static Adjustment	
1	2.73	
2	8.12	
3	10.70	
4	5.78	
5	16.84	
6	6.90	
7	12.92	
8	14.75	
9	0.00	(.004)
10	5.49	
11	8.53	
12	2.99	
13	5.94	
14	5.30	

Figure 28
Static Adjustments In Descending Order

Fund	StaticAdjustment
5	16.84
8	14.75
7	12.92
3	10.70
11	8.53
2	8.12
6	6.90
13	5.94
4	5.78
10	5.49
14	5.30
12	2.99
1	2.73
9	0.00

Figure 29 adds the relevant information from Figure 24 (reported and true returns for the various funds) to Figure 27.

Figure 29
Returns (Reported and True) and Static Adjustment

Fund	Rate of Return		Static Adj.
	Reported	True	
1	22.99	22.99	2.73
2	48.80	45.67	8.12
3	7.92	3.48	10.70
4	13.19	15.66	5.78
5	12.71	20.77	16.84
6	33.55	34.45	6.90
7	18.13	24.25	12.92
8	12.40	19.51	14.75
9	23.21	22.82	0.00
10	49.59	47.55	5.49
11	76.20	68.91	8.53
12	10.47	11.93	2.99
13	71.79	62.19	5.94
14	8.93	11.03	5.30

From Figure 29, we see that the three funds with the biggest negative difference between reported and true returns (i.e., the three funds with the greatest level of under-reported returns) had the largest positive static adjustments. This seems to provide further evidence that those particular funds did indeed greatly understate the interim rates of return. Also, the two funds with the smallest difference between reported and true returns had the two smallest necessary static adjustments.

Finally, we present the static adjustments for each fund as a percentage of the reported and true rates of return. The results are shown as Figure 30.

Figure 30
Static Adjustment as Percentage of Reported and True Return

Fund	Rate of Return			Static Adj. as a % of:	
	Reported	True	Static Adj.	Reported	True
1	22.99	22.99	2.73	11.87%	11.87%
2	48.8	45.67	8.12	16.64%	17.78%
3	7.92	3.48	10.7	135.10%	307.47%
4	13.19	15.66	5.78	43.82%	36.91%
5	12.71	20.77	16.84	132.49%	81.08%
6	33.55	34.45	6.9	20.57%	20.03%
7	18.13	24.25	12.92	71.26%	53.28%
8	12.4	19.51	14.75	118.95%	75.60%
9	23.21	22.82	0	0.00%	0.00%
10	49.59	47.55	5.49	11.07%	11.55%
11	76.2	68.91	8.53	11.19%	12.38%
12	10.47	11.93	2.99	28.56%	25.06%
13	71.79	62.19	5.94	8.27%	9.55%
14	8.93	11.03	5.3	59.35%	48.05%

In only one case was the static adjustment negligible. For the other thirteen funds the static adjustment was, on average, more than 50% of both the reported returns (51.47%) and true returns (54.66%). For only one of those funds was the adjustment less than 10% of the reported and true returns.

The only consideration for an investor in an alternative investment fund is how much money is contributed compared to how much money is received in return. During the lifetime of the fund an alternative asset manager will often market a new fund. An investor's decision as to whether or not to invest in the new fund depends largely on how well the existing fund is performing. This has led many skeptics to conclude that alternative investment managers have an incentive to and, in fact, do overstate the interim rates of return. What we have found, from an examination of an extremely small sample, is that alternative asset funds tend to understate the reported returns.

-12-
RISK-FREE RATE OF RETURN

There are many calculations that use a risk-free rate of return, such as the capital asset pricing model and the Black-Scholes model of options pricing. For many years the risk-free rate of return has been defined as the return on near-term maturity US Treasury Bills. The financial strength of the US, along with the short duration of the security (usually three months or less), makes the return on the Treasury Bill an excellent proxy for a risk-free rate of return.

There are essentially two main risks faced by an investor in fixed income securities, whether they are government debt or corporate bonds – the risk of bankruptcy by the borrower and the risk of a rise in the market rate of interest, which would lower the market value of the debt. The financial strength of the US mitigates the risk of bankruptcy (though after a debt-rating downgrade in 2011 some may want to question this assertion, but I still believe that US Government Securities are safe) and the short maturity of the Treasury bill mitigates the risk of a rise in the market rate. Since the holder can redeem the bonds at maturity for face value, and the duration is generally three months or less, the holder does not need to worry about any change in the value of the debt.

What we know: The risk-free rate of return still exists

The risk-free rate is important for a number of reasons. As a metric, the risk-free rate is used in a number of calculations. Throughout the years, the risk-free return has been the short duration US Treasury bill. A chart of the weekly market rate on the 3-month US Treasury bill[16] is shown as Figure 31.

---

[16]Downloaded from http://www.federalreserve.gov/releases/h15/data.htm, November 22, 2011

Figure 31
Weekly Market Rate on the 3-Month US Treasury Bill

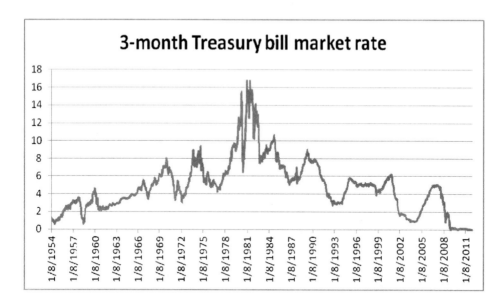

Currently, the risk-free rate of return is near zero (.01%). And from the graph, it is apparent that the risk-free rate of return has been near zero for a number of years. While it is not the same thing as saying there is no risk-free rate of return, using a rate of zero (or near zero) has virtually the same effect.

If having a risk-free rate is important in setting a baseline for what an investor could receive with no risk involved, then having a risk-free rate of zero (or near zero) for an extended period essentially says that there is no risk-free rate in the current market. Any return above .01% will involve having to tolerate risk.

Another consideration is the calculation of the return. Since a return is comprised of a yield (cash flow) combined with a change in market value (capital appreciation/depreciation), the concept of the risk-free return might not really be what is implied. Perhaps we should be contemplating a risk-free yield. The yield is not affected by holding gains and losses (changes in the value of the debt due to market rate changes). The yield is simply the interest divided by the price paid to acquire the debt and does not fluctuate with changes in the value of the debt (the way the return would). So, perhaps we should say there is no risk-free return, but there is a risk-free yield.

-13-
LIQUIDITY PREMIUMS

Investors love to talk about liquidity premiums. A liquidity premium is the premia required by an investor to compensate them for the inability to access their capital for some period of time. The longer the lack of access, the higher the liquidity premium. I cannot tell you how many times I have heard investors say they did not make an investment because they did not feel they were going to be adequately compensated for the liquidity they were giving up.

When contemplating a particular investment, every potential investor thinks about the various elements of the return – return on investment, plus additional returns for the risk undertaken and liquidity given up. This parsing of the return into different components is entirely appropriate and leads to better investment decisions. Understanding the elements of a particular investment's return and being able to attribute the return to the different characteristics of the investment, leads to improved portfolio management. Since there are often multiple alternatives for any one investment decision, this deconstructing of the overall expected return allows the investments to be compared on a more granular basis.

Liquidity is an important consideration in selecting a manager or fund and being able to quantify the value to the investor of the liquidity foregone and compare it to the premia embedded in the overall return makes the decision a rational process. There certainly seems to be little point in agreeing to not have access to your capital for long periods unless you were getting compensated for it.

What we know: Liquidity premiums exist and their value can be calculated

It would be easy to identify and calculate liquidity premiums if the same investment were offered in liquid and illiquid forms. An example of that would be a situation where a given manager offered an investment in a format that allowed daily liquidity, and also in a format that only offered annual liquidity (or liquidity on a more extended basis). Both formats would have to invest in exactly the same securities, in the same proportions, purchased at the same time at the same price. The liquidity premium would be represented by a higher return (or a lower management fee, which results in a higher return net of fees). There are few, if any, investments offered in both liquid and illiquid forms (I can think of none, but leave the door open for any reader that has encountered such an investment). That makes discerning a liquidity premium an after-the-fact exercise. The liquidity premium will be calculated at the end of a particular period, as the investment return, risk premium and liquidity premium are partitioned from the total return provided.

The typical holdings in a limited partnership form of investment would ordinarily be invested in things like real estate, venture capital and private equity, the purchase of oil wells, gas reserves and timberland. The nature of what is being invested in determines the need for the lack of access to getting one's money out, and the illiquidity is essentially part and parcel of the return. Calculating the liquidity premium after the fact has elements of being arbitrary and capricious. Hedge funds might hold investments that are generally liquid, but the nature of their investing (use of derivatives, leverage, etc.) requires that their process for providing liquidity to investors be limited, planned and with substantial notice, hence the common "once per year with 30 – 90 days notice."

If I met a fund manager who said their fund paid a 3% liquidity premium plus or minus the return on the assets, then I would buy the concept of the liquidity premium. But this hasn't happened. The liquidity premium seems to be an invention from the investor's side of the table. The investor determines what they think the liquidity premium to be, and either invests or doesn't. This premium is neither guaranteed, disclosed, nor able to be calculated a priori. It is only some investor's estimate. And besides, if it really existed it would be called an "illiquidity premium."

-14-
RISK PREMIUMS

Risk premiums are similar to liquidity premiums – an amount additive to the investment return that compensates an investor for additional considerations involved in the investment. Risk premia is the additional return required by an investor to compensate them for the additional risk of the investment. The more risk an investor is willing undertake, the higher the return they will demand.

Most institutional investors are not risk-averse; they just want to be compensated for the risk they are taking. Perhaps it might be more accurate to say that institutional investors are averse to risks that they are not compensated for. As fiduciaries and custodians of a portfolio, it is a reasonable expectation that they would be compensated in a manner commensurate for the risks involved. They have a responsibility to assess the level of risk and quantify the additional return required.

There are investments that involve higher risks and provide higher returns. There are those investments that involve higher risks without providing a commensurately higher return. A successful investor can differentiate between the two. There are also investments that entail significant risks and provide lower returns. The failed investor cannot differentiate these investments from any other.

What we know: Risk premiums exist and their value can be calculated

Risk premiums only exist if they can be calculated prior to the investment. They cannot be. Risk premiums can certainly be estimated, but with no sense of specification. In a retrospective manner risk premia is attributed based on overall market or sector performance. This results in a meaningless metric.

The logic underlying the concept of risk premiums is also problematic. It inherently says that an investor looking for a higher return would look to riskier investments and therefore demand a premium for the risk they are taking. The premium is already part and parcel of the higher return – it is not something that exists separately.

No investment exists that I know of that provides a guaranteed risk premium. The return that results from any investment includes all aspects and elements of the return. The idea that a return can be parceled into components usually requires assumptions that are not often valid.

Whenever parsing returns, for risk, for liquidity, for sector, no matter which particular portion is being attributed, the underlying assumption is that there is a relevant figure that represents what the investment would have done without the additional considerations of risk, liquidity, etc. There is no reason to believe that this figure is relevant or appropriate. Similar to the issues of using a benchmark, this broadly devised figure is assumed to be the baseline of all similar investments and any variability is ascribed to the differentiators under discussion. If you do not accept this relevant figure, then all the ascribed components no longer exist. You are simply left with a return for a particular investment that is inclusive of all nuances of the investment.

It seems to me that most investors like to feel that they utilize a rational process for investing. Nothing is more rational than detailed calculations that lead to definitive actions. To the investor who says that they didn't make an investment because they were not going to be compensated for the risk, I ask what the return of that fund will be next year (no one knows until the year has elapsed) and what portion of that return represents the risk premium (no one ever knows that until they develop a model using assumptions that are highly challengeable).

-15-
<u>ALPHA</u>

Investing has become a quantified science. And there is nothing more scientific than using Greek letters to represent variables. In an investing context, "alpha" is defined as the return provided by an investment above a baseline. This baseline is usually an appropriate benchmark which should be based on the strategy employed by the investment fund, and related to the type of investing done by the fund. Often indices are used as benchmarks, and the index chosen is usually the one closest to the strategy. Indices are usually low cost, widely available and broad market, so using it as a benchmark certainly seems reasonable. A fund that invests in US large cap securities might use the S&P 500 as a benchmark. Alpha would be defined as the amount by which the investment outperformed the S&P 500. Since the investor could have gotten the return provided by the S&P 500 by investing in the index, the manager has to provide a return above that (net of fees).

Alpha also is sometimes defined as a risk-adjusted return provided by an investment above an appropriate benchmark. Risk-adjustment can be based on any of a number factors, such as volatility. In some ways it is a more robust measure of the manager's contribution.

No matter how you define alpha or how complicated you get in its calculation, it is the performance of a fund relative to something else – in most cases a benchmark that is based on an index. This allows an investor to ascribe what acumen the manager has, what the manager has brought to the table, and the value-added benefit of hiring the manager. Since anyone can invest in the index, to justify their fee, the manager has to provide a return at or above the benchmark on a net-of-fee basis.

What we know: Alpha exists and is quantifiable

Investing is largely a zero-sum game. For every winner there is a loser. If all investors start buying stocks today, and sell tomorrow, the sum of all gains will be canceled out by the sum of the losses, on a market basis. However, we don't all start investing at the same time and we don't all stop investing at the same time. We enter the picture at different points of time. And the market does not come to an end (at least it hasn't, yet). So, we have different time horizons, and different beginning and ending points. At any point in time investing is not a zero sum game. Only after it is all said and done will it be a zero sum game. So does alpha exist or not?

As defined, alpha is a singular calculation made at a particular point in time, and therefore offers a sense of being concrete and knowable. In some respects then, it represents the sole reason for hiring a manager. Seasoned investors will generally agree that alpha can exist in some markets more than others. It is very hard to find alpha for US equity funds. It is easier to find alpha in international and emerging markets.

The reason it is difficult to find alpha in US equity funds is because of how developed the market is, the growth of mutual funds and ETFs, the liquidity present and the variety of investor (retail, institutional, sovereign, etc.). It is easier to find alpha when the market is expanding because new participants are entering the market and there is variability in when the participants exit the market. From the beginning of a market to the end of the market, the sum of all gains and losses will be zero. In calculating alpha we break up the history of a market into a much shorter time horizon. An immature market lends itself to having alpha, whereas a mature market does not.

Alpha in an emerging market may be nothing more that the paper gains (unrealized gains) a particular fund has in their holdings. Alpha should not be based on unrealized gains because it could give an inaccurate assessment of how a manager is performing. Selling a holding at the right time is also part of the manager's job. In small markets (such as some frontier markets and some smaller emerging markets) a sale by a manager might destroy the market value of the holdings and drive the price of the security down if they are a substantial holder of the security (a market-maker, or worse, if they are the market).

Unrealized gains can carry over for an extended period, providing "alpha" and performance fees for many years. Assuming that the fund invests in liquid securities should mean that they can turn the unrealized gain into a realized gain at any time. It seems to me that if the unrealized prior gains on a particular security are never realized then the manager should have to recalculate all prior returns, removing the contribution of this security. Somehow, twenty quarters of alpha tends not to be reversed by one quarter of negative return in the minds of managers and investors, even when the previous gains are reversed in the one quarter.

Unlike model based valuations, a fund that invests in liquid securities truly does have a valuation that is reliably accurate and verifiable. But if the manager doesn't realize the value though a sale, then all prior return calculations are meaningless. The prior return and associated alpha are "woulda, shoulda, coulda." But didn't. Alpha should not represent what could have happened (if I sold) but represent what did happen (I didn't sell).

-16-
INTERNATIONAL INVESTING

As the world has gotten smaller, the emergence of non-US investments as an allocated portion of an investor's portfolio has dramatically increased. There are a variety of investments that include companies that are located in foreign countries (anything outside of the US), companies whose stocks are listed on foreign exchanges and companies that make their money from a variety of different markets (developed countries, emerging markets and frontier markets). The presence of foreign markets even has an effect on US domiciled companies. According to Goldman Sachs, in 2009 30% of the revenues of the companies that comprise the S&P 500 were from overseas.[17]

There are over 1,000 mutual funds you can select from that invest solely in international equities (securities of companies domiciled outside the US). Add in ETFs, managers and their related funds, global funds (which include securities of companies domiciled both within and without the US) and the variety of fixed income alternatives and multi-strategy funds, and it is easy to see that there are many investment choices on an international scale. In 1969 US companies represented almost 71% of the global index.[18] In 2011 this share had decreased to 42%.[19]

Simultaneous with the increase in investment choices has been the increase in allocation to international investments by institutional investors. During the period 1999 through 2009, US investors increased their allocation to

---

[17]Goldman Sachs Global ECS Research (S&P 500 Index data), 04.23.10, shown as Exhibit 7 in "The Case for Global Investing," Newton
[18]"Investment Analysis and Portfolio Management," Frank K. Reilly and Keith C. Brown, 2002, shown as Exhibit 4 in "The Case for Global Investing," Newton
[19]FactSet, MSCI All Countries Index, shown as Exhibit 4 in "The Case for Global Investing," Newton

international equities and bonds by 31% (in 1999 international equities and bonds presented a combined 13% of the portfolio, in 2009 17%).

As explained by some fund managers that I have spoken with, a good company is a good company whether it is located in Europe, the US or Asia. This has some intuitive appeal. Analyzing a company utilizes the same fundamentals wherever the company might be domiciled. A strong analytical skill set should be portable from domestic investments to international investments.

Many investment managers have chosen to concentrate in either domestic or international companies, mostly as a result of scale. To effectively deliver returns in any geography requires expertise and local knowledge. This comes from devotion of time and resources, and that is easier attained through specialization. Trying to be expert in too many geographies can result in spreading a firm's manpower too thin. Larger entities have the potential to be global rather than concentrated in a particular locale by virtue of having more resources to deploy.

Some investment managers focus on sectors regardless of geography. They believe they can effectively analyze companies no matter where they are located or from where a majority of their sales are derived because they understand what the company does and how the sector operates. They believe it is easier to obtain any relevant local knowledge to supplement their industry knowledge then it would be to have local knowledge and try to obtain the industry knowledge.

What we know: Securities are appropriately classified as international

When it comes to the categorization of international securities, I have experienced a wide range of practice. Most classify securities as either domestic or international based on where they are domiciled, others based on which index the security is included in, and to a much lesser extent, some classify based on where the company derives its revenues. All methods of classification can be justified, as well as criticized. If the purpose of asset allocation is to group investments with similar risk characteristics, then it would seem the least used method, classification based on revenue sourcing, would be most appropriate since this arguably provides a better grouping of companies with similar risks. From the manager's perspective classifying companies based on which index they belong to has some favorable aspects – this provides a closer alignment between their holdings and the benchmark (index) against which they will be evaluated.

There is no right answer about how companies should be classified. But it is something every investor should inquire about. Often times the reasoning used in classification can provide some insight. The one answer I would not think acceptable is that the manager had not considered classification as an issue or that they believe it to be irrelevant.

Managers are the investment experts and investors hire them because of their expertise, experience and knowledge base, which is beyond what the investor possesses. An international company included in an international portfolio would be analyzed and vetted by the manager's team. The manager should be experts in the company, the industry and the country. But that might not be good enough – if there is a concentration in sales (meaning that a large percentage of sales are to a small number of customers) they may also have to be expert in the customers or customs of the company. Without understanding that some companies are classified as international (based on domicile), but are really US companies (based on sales), can skew an investor's asset allocation. In an extreme, an investor might be allocated 50% US and 50% international and find that 100% of their portfolio is highly sensitive to the US economy. This defeats the purpose of asset allocation.

What we know: Returns on international funds are a result of the manager's investment decisions

Managers are evaluated based on the returns they produce, and frequently evaluated based on the returns they produce relative to an agreed-upon benchmark. When investing outside one's geography, one also tends to invest outside one's local currency. When this happens the foreign investment has to be converted to the home currency. In making this conversion there is the possibility of foreign exchange gains and losses. Good investment decisions, that is, those purchases of securities that had a resultant increase in value, can be offset by a negative move in the currency those securities are denominated in. Likewise, bad investment decisions (purchasing securities of companies that have lost value) can be masked by positive movements in the foreign currency relative to the home currency. And, of course, good investments can be made even better by positive currency fluctuations just as bad investments can be made worse by negative currency fluctuations.

Some managers hedge the currency exposure. In doing so, their returns are closer to representing the results of their investment decisions. Other managers choose not to hedge the currency exposure. Their returns are reflective of their investment decisions combined with foreign exchange adjustments.

It is not difficult to segregate the investment return from the return provided by foreign exchange for any single period. Over multiple time horizons and multiple currencies, this gets more complex. Securities held in a fund are bought at different times, at differing prices and in differing quantities. So, keeping track is a tedious task if the fund is not set up with this in mind. Most fund computer systems should be able to track foreign exchange gains and losses. Whether the manager chooses to do this, and if they do, whether they choose to disclose it, is another matter. My experience is that I will tend to see more disclosure about foreign currency effects when the exchange rate hurt the return, and less disclosure when the foreign currency exchange helped the return. Until foreign currency gains and losses are parsed from an international fund's return, an investor will never have a true idea of how the manager has done.

Some examples might prove helpful. The monthly return for the MSCI AC World ex US was 6.69% in January 2012.[20] Of this, 2.09% was attributed to foreign currency. Foreign currency represented over 30% of the index's gain. For the quarter ended in January 2012 the index returned -.24%, with -1.82% attributable to foreign currency. Had it not been for currency, the index would have been positive for the quarter.

The same holds true for emerging markets. The MSCI EM index returned 11.24% for January 2012, with 4.28% of the return attributed to foreign currency. Foreign currency was responsible for 38% of the index's return for the month.

While the importance of foreign currency to returns will vary greatly period to period, the idea is that it should not be overlooked. An international manager is going to generate returns comprised of the return on their security selections as well as the returns attributable to foreign currency exchange. Segregating the return allows the investor to determine how well the manager does with each, and whether the manager appropriately hedges the foreign currency when necessary.

---

[20]This, as well as the data that follows, comes from the "Record Currency Management Monthly US Factsheet," a publication of Record Currency Management, January 2012.

-17-

TAIL-RISK HEDGING

The financial crisis of the latter part of the first decade of the new millennium (starting a little before 2008 and ending a little after) brought new consideration to the volatility of markets and portfolios. In some months it was not unusual to see investments decline by 50%. Some managers felt that the market had ridden a long path to its current valuation and were concerned that the market was due for a fall. These managers used a portion of the fund expenses to protect the fund from tail-risk (a significant and severe, though infrequent, event). They generally used options to provide their tail-risk protection.

I know some investment managers that were able to significantly dampen market declines in their portfolio by the gains made on the hedges they had in place. For a relatively low cost they received a sizable payoff. The manager's foresight kept a bad situation from becoming a catastrophic one. The fund may have lost money, but not nearly as much as they would have lost had they not had the hedge in place.

The common consensus is that tail-risk hedges are cheap when you don't need them and expensive when you do. The managers that had the vision to buy the hedges when they were cheap (and thought unnecessary) effectively protected their fund.

Investors have been looking into developing tail-risk strategies for their portfolio. Seeing twenty years' of gains wiped out in a short time span is a sobering experience.

What we know: Investors should protect their portfolios from tail-risk

The term "investor" is not a one-size fits all term. Some investors select individual securities and do not use managers. Others use a combination of outside managers as well as an in-house investment office. Some entities exclusively select managers, while others outsource all elements of portfolio management.

For investors that make their own investment decisions, it may be entirely prudent for them to evaluate and manage the tail-risk in their portfolio. For investors that select managers, that decision is quite different.

Managers are hired to analyze potential investments, size holdings, rebalance and position their portfolio in varying market conditions. They run and have full control and discretion over their portfolios. While they may share the list of the fund's holdings with investors, this is a static indicator that is often provided infrequently, even if regularly. Some managers allow real-time, online access to the portfolio holdings so that investors can see what is in the portfolio at any point in time. And separate accounts allow the investor to see the holdings.

Even with the most up-to-date, open access, only the manager is privy to any plans that may involve shaping the portfolio in the future. The investor might know what securities are in the investment fund, but not what the plans are for holding, divesting or adding to the position, or what stocks may be purchased in the near future. The investor is not in a position to be able to adequately determine how to protect the portfolio from tail-risk, even if they wanted to. The manager is in a position to place a hedge against tail-risk, but not the investor.

What the investor is in a position to do is to place a hedge on the market (as opposed to a hedge against the portfolio or any investment within the portfolio). In this regard, the hedge becomes a separate and distinct speculative investment. Tail-risk hedges are about market price movement instead of protecting what the portfolio consists of. Hedges not strictly related to portfolio holdings are not hedges against portfolio declines but discrete investments. Investors have to consider whether this is something they are capable of evaluating and investing in. If they decide it is a prudent investment for their portfolio then they should do it, recognizing that they are not making a hedge with the purpose of protecting their portfolio, but investing in an option that bets against the market.

Semantically it may seem similar, since if the market drops the hedge pays off, which offset any loss in the investment funds held by the entity. But investors invest in subsets of the market and a more efficient hedge will protect against drops in the subsets. A hedge against the S&P 500 that does not pay off because the S&P 500 rose does not imply that the investor's portfolio went up.

Investors that try to protect their portfolio from tail-risk should recognize that they are evaluating and making an individual investment on their own. If the investor has the competence and capacity to do this, then they should. Otherwise they should realize that there is a reason why they have structured their investing model the way they have, why they utilize the services of outside parties (consultants, advisors, managers) and they should not deviate from that model.

-18-
ASSET ALLOCATION

It has been said that there are three decisions a typical institutional investor makes – asset allocation, manager selection and choice of vehicle[21]. It is no coincidence that asset allocation is listed first. Through the years, asset allocation has been shown to be a critical component of risk mitigation and return optimization. Asset allocation is usually reserved as an investment committee decision, even in institutions that use consultants and hire managers. The targets and bands in the asset allocation framework are the purview of the fiduciaries that are ultimately responsible for the performance of the portfolio.

There are different levels of investor sophistication, even among institutional investors. Some institutional investors have built-out investment offices and do their own research and security selection. Most institutional investors tend to use some form of outside consulting, whether it be limited to due diligence or for more extensive services. In all cases, some form of asset allocation is a focal point and critical element of the management of the portfolio.

Asset allocation used to be a rather standard exercise involving a framework that was fairly typical among investors. Classic asset allocation has used segregations such as:

Domestic equity
International equity
Fixed income

---

[21]Most include asset allocation and manager selection as the two decisions most investors make. I like to add the third term, vehicle selection, because this is an important choice for the investor – whether they prefer a separate account or commingled structure, for instance.

And further segregations such as:

Domestic equity
    Large Cap
    Mid Cap
    Small Cap

International Equity
    Developed markets
    Emerging markets
    Frontier markets

Fixed income
    Government securities
    Corporate securities

And further segregations, such as:

Domestic equity
    Large Cap
        Value
        Growth
    Mid Cap
        Value
        Growth
    Small Cap
        Value
        Growth

And so on. The gradations of how the asset classes may be broken down are seemingly endless. You could get as granular as needed or desired.

Recently, some investors have moved away from the classic method of asset allocation and started using different frameworks. Some differentiate the asset classes by allocating based on:

- Return-enhancing (for growth)
- Risk-minimizing (for stability)

- Hedges (to protect against inflation)[22]

Or utilizing risk-based asset allocation:

- Interest rate risk
- Market risk
- Active risk[23]

Asset allocation is a pervasive tool among institutional investors. The process of rebalancing is based on an evaluation of how the current asset allocation compares to the target (policy) asset allocation. Shifts are made as appropriate, to adjust the security holdings to better align with the approved asset allocations (targets and bands).

Asset allocation has developed and evolved, and has remained a critical piece of portfolio management. Asset allocation serves as an overriding management tool in evaluating where to deploy investment capital, what investments should continue to be held and providing a control to avoid concentrations in sectors and geography.

What we know: The asset classes used in asset allocation are appropriate

Asset allocation is only as good as the asset classes used and the accuracy of the classification of securities into those classes. Investing has gotten more complex at the same time as the world has gotten smaller. Most companies are transacting business across borders and there are more types of securities to invest in. This has made placing securities into the proper asset classes more difficult. Asset allocation only works if the investor understands why they are doing it, what the function and purpose of asset allocation is and what the groupings represent.

Would you place a company that was located in the US, listed on a US stock exchange but made 100% of its sales in Europe into a domestic equity asset class or an international asset class? How about a European company, listed on a European exchange but where all their sales come from the US – would that

---

[22]University of Connecticut Foundation, as quoted, http://www.foundation.uconn.edu/press-release-2010-10-uconn-foundation-top-nonprofit.html.
[23]Robert Litterman, "Quantitative Investing," Ibbotson Asset Allocation Conference, March 2008

be included in the international asset class allocation or included within domestic equity?

There is no easy answer. In trying to achieve a proper match between the desired asset allocation scheme and where the investments should be categorized at any particular time requires that the securities be placed in the proper classes based on some criteria. Doing so has become more difficult and often results in the use of judgment.

If the investor is using asset allocation to group securities based upon risk characteristics or how the security will behave in differing market scenarios, then that should drive the classifications used in asset allocation groupings. I would suggest that even where that is the intent it is often not how it is actually done. Classification is frequently based on domicile, which may not be more effective in achieving the benefits of asset allocation then categorization by alphabetizing. Either one may have no relationship to the purpose and structure of asset allocation.

From the previous chapter (on whether the market went to 1) we saw that during the financial crisis all US domestic equity and developed international equity were highly correlated. It might very well be that we are in a paradigm shift where there is no functional utility to splitting domestic equity and international developed equity. If they truly behave as one asset class then they represent diversification but not non-correlation.

Asset allocation serves the purpose of helping to direct where an investor should make investments. The structure can be very different from investor to investor. The recent developments show a greater range of vision when looking at the investment palate. I believe there are yet more ways to do asset allocation.

We invest not for today, but for tomorrow. To that end, what is important is what the market will do, and how it will do it. I look at tomorrow as being comprised of one of three possibilities – a rising market, a steady-state market and a declining market. Within these three possibilities there are those securities that will do well in each. I would further divide these securities into those that are high volatility, medium volatility and low volatility.

I would allocate the portfolio based on how I saw the future, keeping in mind that I would want to be able to allocate to all three market possibilities and have the flexibility to adjust the portfolio as the broader vision changes. This would inform the liquidity needs of the portfolio.

If I felt that the market was rising I might allocate say 65% of the portfolio to securities that perform well in rising markets, and allocate among the levels of volatility depending on my return needs. I might allocate 20% to securities that perform well in steady-state markets, and perhaps the balance (15%) to securities that perform well in declining markets. Again, I would choose among high, medium or low volatility companies depending on return needs. The stronger my conviction was, the higher the allocation to that type of market.

This allocation scheme is not one I have seen before, but it makes sense to me. If the market is rising, pick securities that do well in rising markets. Who cares what sector they operate in (as long as the portfolio does not become concentrated). If the market is declining, pick securities that do well in declining markets (it shouldn't matter where they are located, as long as no concentration exists). I simply put it forward as another alternative in thinking about different ways to provide a framework for asset allocation.

-19-
MANAGER PERFORMANCE

A general distinction can be made in investing between "growth" and "value" investors. Value investors look for stocks that are undervalued according to a proprietary algorithm or fundamental analysis. Growth investors look for stocks of companies that should have revenue increases beyond the average company, and given the market's predilection to reward growth, that company's stock should appreciate at a higher rate relative to the broader market. Each model has its fans and detractors. Retail investors often invest with a strategy that can best be defined as a momentum strategy – they buy stocks in a rising market and sell during a declining market. This can also be cynically called "buying high and selling low."

For investors that select managers, rather than securities, there is a similar process employed – hiring successful managers. Managers that have a recent run that places them in the top quartile tend to do better at attracting new clients and capital. Perennial bottom quartile managers will generally lose capital and eventually wind up having to shutter their fund.

There is a growing body of literature that finds new(er) managers tend to perform better than managers with longer track records. I tend to find these studies/papers/reports creditable, but not because newer managers are better investors. I believe it is because it is easier to be successful with less capital to deploy - you have the luxury to select only those best ideas. Managers who are successful and wind up with larger pools of capital to invest, it seems to me, can exhaust their best ideas with the result of having to invest in their second and third tier of best ideas.

Every investment comes with the qualifier "past performance is not an indication of future performance." And yet, investors tend to flock to the best performers of the recent past. Without any reliable data about future performance, investors tend to utilize past performance, because this is all they have.

What we know: Manager performance is repeatable and predictable

If you ask investors what the statement "past performance is not an indication of future performance" means, I would bet that they say "the great performance of yesterday may not be repeated tomorrow" or something to that effect. It is a warning that the past may not be a good predictor of the future. I do think that is the intent of the warning, a limiter on what the past investment performance can be expected to tell us about the future. Investors have no information about the future, only what the fund or manager has done in the past. They will tend to place more reliance on the only quantified information that exists.

I don't think many people would say that the phrase also implies that poor performance may not be repeated. A second or third quartile firm may be the next top quartile firm. Firms whose performance has been lacking (such as a second or third tier firm) but who have good processes, ideas, controls, people, intellectual capital, etc., may not be condemned to an ever-declining ranking or a ranking that continues in the lower quartiles.

These lagging firms may have lost capital or have an inability to raise new capital relative to top quartile firms, which, if you believe that smaller is better, gives them a competitive advantage in future performance. It would not be unusual for an investor to look at long-term performance in deciding which manager to hire. I took a list of the top 40 managers based on 10 years' worth of returns in a given strategy, with the idea that an investor who wishes to invest in that strategy might indeed consult such a list.

I then looked at the top 40 managers in the strategy a few years later, based on one year's returns. Not one of the original 40 repeats. In the original list, of the 40 managers, 17 managed assets that had over $1 billion in that fund. In the later list only 6 managers had over $1 billion in their fund.

While certainly not definitive, this at least presents some food for thought that performance is not necessarily repeatable. I am sure there are those managers that do perform on a consistent basis, year after year. However, given the distribution of managers that have performed for X number of years, a certain percentage of them will cease performing at that level. Which managers will continue at that level and which will not is hard to predict.

128

In an ideal world, investors would hire the managers that would do well once hired. Even (or especially) when the manager has performed to the expectations of investors, the investor needs to consider how long to continue to stay invested. Just as I suggest that hiring a manager that has under-performed in the past may be a prudent move, getting out of a successful investment may be equally as prudent.

-20-
LONG-TERM INVESTING

With a primary goal of perpetuity, institutional investors are clearly long-term investors. They have a long-term perspective and do not make decisions based on short-term phenomena. Nor do they have knee-jerk reactions to system shocks. Having a long view allows these investors to ride out market cycles, not make rash decisions. They can avoid pressure to maximize short-term returns.

That institutional investors usually have a substantial allocation to alternative investments, which are largely illiquid limited partnerships with extended durations for payback, is tangible evidence of their commitment to long-term investing. They use evaluative criteria with calculations performed over 1-year, 5-year and 10-year periods comparing them to benchmarks and peer groups over similar extended periods, which offers further evidence of the commitment to a long-term focus.

This long-term view also allows these entities to strategically be concerned with only permanent paradigm shifts. It frees the institutional investor from making judgments about short-cycles and avoids market timing.

What we know: Institutional investors have a long-term perspective

If only the above was true. While I do think that institutional investors believe they are long-term focused, I don't think the reality plays out quite that way. Let's say there was an investment fund that over a 15-year period returned 10% compounded annually (which is not to say that every year had a 10% return). So, you invest with this manager. During the first year the fund loses 25%. During the second year the fund loses 25%. Do you stay with this manager? Do you divest and move on? A reasonable question concerning the 15-year results would be whether they had consecutive years of 25% drawdowns during that run. Let's say they did. Do you stay with this manager?

An investor who takes the long view would stay. I am not so sure I would. If you decided to stay, how long a leash would the manager have? Would the next losing quarter be it for them? Any reasonable investor would be worried.

In any time period, anomalous results force the question about whether times have changed. Is the manager too large to generate the same returns? Did the manager lose talented staff? Have they lost their touch? Maybe the previous run was just a product of luck. There is no end to the list of questions the investor can develop.

Another indication that I believe points to institutional investors not being so long-term as they would have us believe, is that while they calculate returns over a variety of periods, my experience is that focus is often placed on the 1-year return. Longer term returns are mentioned when the 1-year return is below expectation. But when the 1- year return is above expectation, the longer-term returns are seldom mentioned when the long-term results were less than satisfactory.

I do believe that institutional investors have tried to set up their portfolios for the long-term, but their decisions and actions will largely be informed by the short-term. Whenever the impetus for decision-making is current events, the focus has shifted from the long-term. A long-term investor would try to put the current events in the context of what it means for the long-term, but it is my sense that decisions are made allowing the current events to stand on their own.

-21-
SMALLER, BUT NO
<u>LESS IMPORTANT ISSUES</u>

There are other topics that are worthy of discussion, but just didn't make it into a chapter. Perhaps because they didn't lend themselves to the "what we know ..." format or maybe because there was just not a lot I wanted to say about them. But I did want to mention them somewhere.

Transparency
Investors often complain about the level of transparency they receive. I separate transparency into two issues – the transparency investors ask for and the transparency investors need. Every investor is different, and there are certainly those that need a high level of transparency. But I would propose that most do not. Investors should receive the level of transparency they need in order to properly manage their portfolio.

This might involve sector or geographic or currency level transparency. It probably does not involve position level transparency. When investors clearly identify and articulate their needs, I have found that managers usually provide the needed transparency without any problems.

Some investors want the most detailed level of transparency simply because it is their money. I do not think they do anyone a service (themselves, fellow investors or the manager) by being insistent on requesting something they don't need, but simply want. If they do need it, then they should be able to access it, but that is probably the rare occasion.

Risk vs. Uncertainty

I think investors often confuse risk and uncertainty. Risk applies to those situations that can be anticipated and quantified. Uncertainty is those times that cannot be identified nor planned for. I have car insurance because of risk, and I have life insurance because of uncertainty.

In financial modeling risk can be incorporated, but uncertainty cannot. Uncertainty can only be given quantitative acknowledgement by the incorporation of a "noise" factor. I previously suggested that 50 – 80% would be appropriate, but I have no justification for that range.

Illiquidity By Design vs. Illiquidity By Circumstance

Some investment options are illiquid by design, and some turn out to be illiquid by circumstance. If you enter an investment knowing that it will be an extended period to receive any funds back, than that is part and parcel of how the fund is managed and will be a major factor in determining the type of investments that the fund can make.

A fund that is supposed to have a level of liquidity (whatever that level is) and turns out to be unable to provide that level, has to be thought of separately from those investments that were not supposed to have liquidity. During the financial crisis I remember investors complaining about their alternative assets and that there was no liquidity associated with them. Well, the investors knew that going into them – the problem was the marketable investments that were supposed to have liquidity and turned out not to.

Socially Responsible (And Mission Related) Investing

I used to think that socially responsible (SRI) and mission related (MRI) investing were bad ideas because they filter out (or filter in, depending on how you do it) some very high performing securities. After further thought, I have changed my mind. SRI and MRI are just another way to parse a very large universe. A manager with a US small cap fund will filter out large cap, mid cap, international developed and emerging markets. Why would someone consider investing with them? Because these managers have expertise in selecting investments within a sector of the investing universe, I believe the same logic can be applied to SRI and MRI. Narrowing the investable universe allows these managers to concentrate on a limited number of companies.

-22-
<u>SO WHAT DO WE DO NOW</u>

In the end, investing is about nothing more than taking money and doing something with it so that you have more money in the future than you had previously. The amount one wants the sum to increase to should be based upon needs. In a lot of ways the return target in the investment policy statement should be based in similar fashion to the return a future retiree needs in order to accumulate the appropriate amount to continue their desired lifestyle.

The more you need to accumulate, the higher the return you need to earn, which will dictate certain types of investments. The less you need, the lower the return that will accomplish your goals, leading to a different set of investment alternatives. The first step in investing is to assess needs. The mission statement of the organization is the place to start, since it represents what the organization has determined to be its purpose. From this, needs can be assessed and quantified, along with any imposed parameters. This gets translated into an investment policy statement.

A typical investment policy statement might start out with a goal of perpetuity. A second goal might be a real X% return, where the "X" represents the spending needs of the organization (either mandated, as in the case of a private foundation; self-imposed as in the case of a university endowment; or by virtue of the benefit the fund is providing, as in the case of a pension plan). The return can either be relative or absolute. There are a few ways to envision absolute and relative returns, but differentiating between the two is probably not all that important for the purpose of description. Let's call what I described above an absolute return.

I would suggest that combining relative and absolute targets within an investment policy statement is inappropriate and counterproductive. The goals

135

of investing are different between the two types of targets and managing a portfolio that attempts to attain a fixed target (absolute return) and a moving target (relative return) is too difficult. It is like the demands of running a marathon and a sprint – both involve running but the demands of each are different and the implication for how you would train for each is different.

Ten years ago an investor could have locked up an 8% return for the next 30 years. If their target return was a 8%, then maybe they should have jumped at the chance. If their investment policy statement also included a section that stated that they should be in the top quartile of peer performance, then they should not have locked up the 8%. I can understand how the 8% might have been derived and how it could relate to the organization's mission. I do not understand how peer comparisons will benefit the organization. Of course, given the return environment over the last number of years the 8% return seems like a good deal – but what happens if the next ten years see a high inflation environment? Suddenly that 8% is not so desirable. The portfolio must maintain some flexibility to incorporate necessary changes to the return.

Once you have determined what the target return is, then you can develop the structure to provide the personnel and expertise. Essentially, this amounts to deciding how much expertise the organization wishes to have internally and then selecting a level of outsourcing appropriate to complement the core strengths and skill sets the organization possesses or will possess. To be successful the institutional investor needs a well-thought out investment policy, the intellectual capital available either in-house or outsourced, and the ability to try and achieve the target return without ego. How many institutional investors worry about peer rankings?

With the people on board (either internally or outsourced) the institutional investor can begin the process of making investments. No matter whether they do risk budgeting, classic asset allocation or some other variation, they will need to make investments. How they go about determining appropriate investments will be guided by their return goals, world view, liquidity needs and access to investment alternatives.

As I outlined earlier, I would not place much stock in long-term correlation metrics. I would assemble a portfolio based on how securities perform in different market environments and I would vary the volatility based on which environment I was in. I would keep liquidity in mind, both to handle surprises and to be able to shift between market environments as needed. I would rebalance as needed, but not more often than that. I have found no investment thesis that works all the time. I have found many that worked, until they didn't.

I believe in reversion to the mean, so I see second quartile managers with long-track records, stable staff and good processes as worthy of consideration. I also believe that consideration should be given to those funds that have spent a long time in the top quartile. Eventually they will attract enough capital to become too big to invest as efficiently as their track record suggests. An obvious caveat is that those funds that have periodically closed because they recognize that they are capacity constrained might be an exception to this.

Hopefully this book provided additional thoughts and considerations regarding what we think we know and those ideas that we hold to be true. Nothing I have written, none of my thoughts, suggestions or recommendations should be construed as truth. Any reader might feel that some deserve further thought, others might decide none do. If there was one concept that gave you a new way to think about investing, then hopefully you feel it was worth your time.

Thanks for reading.

APPENDIX

Appendix 1

	Prices (NAV) A	Prices (NAV) B	Returns A	Returns B	Prices (NAV) A	Prices (NAV) B	Returns A	Returns B	Prices (NAV) A	Prices (NAV) B	Returns A	Returns B
1	100	100			100	100			100	100		
2	110	110	0.10	0.10	110	110	0.10	0.10	110	110	0.10	0.10
3	120	120	0.09	0.09	120	120	0.09	0.09	120	120	0.09	0.09
4	130	80	0.08	-0.33	130	80	0.08	-0.33	130	80	0.08	-0.33
5	140	140	0.08	0.75	140	93	0.08	0.16	140	90	0.08	0.13
6	150	150	0.07	0.07	150	106	0.07	0.14	150	100	0.07	0.11
7	160	160	0.07	0.07	160	119	0.07	0.12	160	110	0.07	0.10
8	170	170	0.06	0.06	170	132	0.06	0.11	170	120	0.06	0.09
9	180	180	0.06	0.06	180	145	0.06	0.10	180	130	0.06	0.08
10	190	190	0.06	0.06	190	158	0.06	0.09	190	140	0.06	0.08
11	200	200	0.05	0.05	200	171	0.05	0.08	200	150	0.05	0.07
12	210	210	0.05	0.05	210	184	0.05	0.08	210	160	0.05	0.07
13	220	220	0.05	0.05	220	197	0.05	0.07	220	170	0.05	0.06
14	230	230	0.05	0.05	230	210	0.05	0.07	230	180	0.05	0.06
15	240	240	0.04	0.04	240	223	0.04	0.06	240	190	0.04	0.06
16	250	250	0.04	0.04	250	236	0.04	0.06	250	200	0.04	0.05
17	260	260	0.04	0.04	260	249	0.04	0.06	260	210	0.04	0.05
18	270	270	0.04	0.04	270	262	0.04	0.05	270	220	0.04	0.05
19	280	280	0.04	0.04	280	276	0.04	0.05	280	230	0.04	0.05
20	290	290	0.04	0.04	290	290	0.04	0.05	290	240	0.04	0.04
corr	0.99		0.14		0.97		-0.10		0.96		-0.11	

Appendix 2

Block 1

	Prices (NAV) C	Prices (NAV) D	Returns C	Returns D
1	100	100		
2	110	110	0.10	0.10
3	120	120	0.09	0.09
4	130	130	0.08	0.08
5	140	140	0.08	0.08
6	150	150	0.07	0.07
7	160	160	0.07	0.07
8	170	170	0.06	0.06
9	180	180	0.06	0.06
10	190	190	0.06	0.06
11	200	200	0.05	0.05
12	210	130	0.05	-0.35
13	220	220	0.05	0.69
14	230	230	0.05	0.05
15	240	240	0.04	0.04
16	250	250	0.04	0.04
17	260	260	0.04	0.04
18	270	270	0.04	0.04
19	280	280	0.04	0.04
20	290	290	0.04	0.04
corr	0.96		0.05	

Block 2

	Prices (NAV) C	Prices (NAV) D'	Returns C	Returns D'
1	100	100		
2	110	110	0.10	0.10
3	120	120	0.09	0.09
4	130	130	0.08	0.08
5	140	140	0.08	0.08
6	150	150	0.07	0.07
7	160	160	0.07	0.07
8	170	170	0.06	0.06
9	180	180	0.06	0.06
10	190	190	0.06	0.06
11	200	200	0.05	0.05
12	210	130	0.05	-0.35
13	220	150	0.05	0.15
14	230	170	0.05	0.13
15	240	190	0.04	0.12
16	250	210	0.04	0.11
17	260	230	0.04	0.10
18	270	250	0.04	0.09
19	280	270	0.04	0.08
20	290	290	0.04	0.07
corr	0.89		0.05	

Block 3

	Prices (NAV) C"	Prices (NAV) D"	Returns C"	Returns D"
1	100	100		
2	110	110	0.10	0.10
3	120	120	0.09	0.09
4	130	130	0.08	0.08
5	140	140	0.08	0.08
6	150	150	0.07	0.07
7	160	160	0.07	0.07
8	170	170	0.06	0.06
9	180	180	0.06	0.06
10	190	190	0.06	0.06
11	200	200	0.05	0.05
12	210	130	0.05	-0.35
13	220	140	0.05	0.08
14	230	150	0.05	0.07
15	240	160	0.04	0.07
16	250	170	0.04	0.06
17	260	180	0.04	0.06
18	270	190	0.04	0.06
19	280	200	0.04	0.05
20	290	210	0.04	0.05
corr	0.76		0.21	

Appendix 3

Panel 1

#	Prices (NAV) E	Prices (NAV) E'	Returns E	Returns E'
1	100	100		
2	110	110	0.10	0.10
3	120	120	0.09	0.09
4	130	130	0.08	0.08
5	140	140	0.08	0.08
6	150	150	0.07	0.07
7	160	160	0.07	0.07
8	170	170	0.06	0.06
9	180	180	0.06	0.06
10	190	190	0.06	0.06
11	200	200	0.05	0.05
12	210	210	0.05	0.05
13	220	220	0.05	0.05
14	230	230	0.05	0.05
15	240	240	0.04	0.04
16	250	250	0.04	0.04
17	260	170	0.04	-0.32
18	270	270	0.04	0.59
19	280	280	0.04	0.04
20	290	290	0.04	0.04
corr		0.94		0.04

Panel 2

#	Prices (NAV) E	Prices (NAV) E'	Returns E	Returns E'
1	100	100		
2	110	110	0.10	0.10
3	120	120	0.09	0.09
4	130	130	0.08	0.08
5	140	140	0.08	0.08
6	150	150	0.07	0.07
7	160	160	0.07	0.07
8	170	170	0.06	0.06
9	180	180	0.06	0.06
10	190	190	0.06	0.06
11	200	200	0.05	0.05
12	210	210	0.05	0.05
13	220	220	0.05	0.05
14	230	230	0.05	0.05
15	240	240	0.04	0.04
16	250	250	0.04	0.04
17	260	170	0.04	-0.32
18	270	210	0.04	0.24
19	280	250	0.04	0.19
20	290	290	0.04	0.16
corr		0.91		0.09

Panel 3

#	Prices (NAV) E'	Prices (NAV) E''	Returns E'	Returns E''
1	100	100		
2	110	110	0.10	0.10
3	120	120	0.09	0.09
4	130	130	0.08	0.08
5	140	140	0.08	0.08
6	150	150	0.07	0.07
7	160	160	0.07	0.07
8	170	170	0.06	0.06
9	180	180	0.06	0.06
10	190	190	0.06	0.06
11	200	200	0.05	0.05
12	210	210	0.05	0.05
13	220	220	0.05	0.05
14	230	230	0.05	0.05
15	240	240	0.04	0.04
16	250	250	0.04	0.04
17	260	170	0.04	-0.32
18	270	180	0.04	0.06
19	280	190	0.04	0.06
20	290	200	0.04	0.05
corr		0.78		0.39

Appendix 4

	Prices (NAV) X	Y	Returns X	Y	Prices (NAV) X'	Y'	Returns X'	Y'	Prices (NAV) X"	Y"	Returns X"	Y"
1	100	100			100	100			100	100		
2	105	105	0.05	0.05	105	105	0.05	0.05	105	105	0.05	0.05
3	110	110	0.05	0.05	110	110	0.05	0.05	110	110	0.05	0.05
4	116	85	0.05	-0.23	116	85	0.05	-0.23	116	85	0.05	-0.23
5	122	122	0.05	0.44	122	91	0.05	0.07	122	89	0.05	0.05
6	128	128	0.05	0.05	128	97	0.05	0.07	128	94	0.05	0.05
7	134	135	0.05	0.05	134	104	0.05	0.07	134	98	0.05	0.05
8	141	141	0.05	0.05	141	111	0.05	0.07	141	103	0.05	0.05
9	148	148	0.05	0.05	148	119	0.05	0.07	148	108	0.05	0.05
10	155	156	0.05	0.05	155	128	0.05	0.07	155	114	0.05	0.05
11	163	163	0.05	0.05	163	136	0.05	0.07	163	120	0.05	0.05
12	171	172	0.05	0.05	171	146	0.05	0.07	171	126	0.05	0.05
13	180	180	0.05	0.05	180	156	0.05	0.07	180	132	0.05	0.05
14	189	189	0.05	0.05	189	167	0.05	0.07	189	138	0.05	0.05
15	198	199	0.05	0.05	198	179	0.05	0.07	198	145	0.05	0.05
16	208	209	0.05	0.05	208	191	0.05	0.07	208	153	0.05	0.05
17	218	219	0.05	0.05	218	205	0.05	0.07	218	160	0.05	0.05
18	229	230	0.05	0.05	229	219	0.05	0.07	229	168	0.05	0.05
19	241	242	0.05	0.05	241	236	0.05	0.08	241	177	0.05	0.05
20	253	254	0.05	0.05	253	253	0.05	0.07	253	186	0.05	0.05
corr	0.99			-0.32	0.97			-0.30	0.96			-0.28

Appendix 5

	Prices (NAV) Y	Prices (NAV) W	Returns Y	Returns W	Prices (NAV) Y'	Prices (NAV) W'	Returns Y"	Returns W	Prices (NAV) Y"	Prices (NAV) W"	Returns Y"	Returns W"
1	100	100	0.05	0.05	100	100	0.05	0.05	100	100	0.05	0.05
2	105	105	0.05	0.05	105	105	0.05	0.05	105	105	0.05	0.05
3	110	110	0.05	0.05	110	110	0.05	0.05	110	110	0.05	0.05
4	116	116	0.05	0.05	116	116	0.05	0.05	116	116	0.05	0.05
5	122	122	0.05	0.05	122	122	0.05	0.05	122	122	0.05	0.05
6	128	128	0.05	0.05	128	128	0.05	0.05	128	128	0.05	0.05
7	134	134	0.05	0.05	134	134	0.05	0.05	134	134	0.05	0.05
8	141	141	0.05	0.05	141	141	0.05	0.05	141	141	0.05	0.05
9	148	148	0.05	0.05	148	148	0.05	0.05	148	148	0.05	0.05
10	155	155	0.05	0.05	155	155	0.05	0.05	155	155	0.05	0.05
11	163	163	0.05	0.05	163	163	0.05	0.05	163	163	0.05	0.05
12	171	110	0.05	-0.32	171	110	0.05	-0.32	171	110	0.05	-0.32
13	180	180	0.05	0.64	180	122	0.05	0.11	180	116	0.05	0.05
14	189	189	0.05	0.05	189	136	0.05	0.11	189	121	0.05	0.05
15	198	198	0.05	0.05	198	150	0.05	0.11	198	127	0.05	0.05
16	208	208	0.05	0.05	208	167	0.05	0.11	208	134	0.05	0.05
17	218	219	0.05	0.05	218	185	0.05	0.11	218	140	0.05	0.05
18	229	230	0.05	0.05	229	206	0.05	0.11	229	147	0.05	0.05
19	241	241	0.05	0.05	241	228	0.05	0.11	241	155	0.05	0.05
20	253	253	0.05	0.05	253	253	0.05	0.11	253	163	0.05	0.05
corr	0.96		-0.09		0.87		0.03		0.61		-0.06	

Appendix 6

	Prices (NAV) T	U	Returns T	U	Prices (NAV) T'	U'	Returns T'	U'	Prices (NAV) T"	U"	Returns T"	U"
1	100	100			100	100			100	100		
2	105	105	0.05	0.05	105	105	0.05	0.05	105	105	0.05	0.05
3	110	110	0.05	0.05	110	110	0.05	0.05	110	110	0.05	0.05
4	116	116	0.05	0.05	116	116	0.05	0.05	116	116	0.05	0.05
5	122	122	0.05	0.05	122	122	0.05	0.05	122	122	0.05	0.05
6	128	128	0.05	0.05	128	128	0.05	0.05	128	128	0.05	0.05
7	134	134	0.05	0.05	134	134	0.05	0.05	134	134	0.05	0.05
8	141	141	0.05	0.05	141	141	0.05	0.05	141	141	0.05	0.05
9	148	148	0.05	0.05	148	148	0.05	0.05	148	148	0.05	0.05
10	155	155	0.05	0.05	155	155	0.05	0.05	155	155	0.05	0.05
11	163	163	0.05	0.05	163	163	0.05	0.05	163	163	0.05	0.05
12	171	171	0.05	0.05	171	171	0.05	0.05	171	171	0.05	0.05
13	180	180	0.05	0.05	180	180	0.05	0.05	180	180	0.05	0.05
14	189	189	0.05	0.05	189	189	0.05	0.05	189	189	0.05	0.05
15	198	198	0.05	0.05	198	198	0.05	0.05	198	198	0.05	0.05
16	208	208	0.05	0.05	208	208	0.05	0.05	208	208	0.05	0.05
17	218	140	0.05	-0.33	218	140	0.05	-0.33	218	140	0.05	-0.33
18	229	229	0.05	0.64	229	171	0.05	0.22	229	147	0.05	0.05
19	241	241	0.05	0.05	241	208	0.05	0.22	241	154	0.05	0.05
20	253	253	0.05	0.05	253	253	0.05	0.21	253	162	0.05	0.05
corr	0.93			0.10	0.89		-0.03	0.68				-0.11

Appendix 7

	Prices (NAV) Δx	Bx	Returns Δx	Bx	Prices (NAV) Δx'	Bx'	Returns Δx'	Bx'	Prices (NAV) Δx"	Bx"	Returns Δx"	Bx"
1	100	100	0.10	0.10	100	100	0.10	0.10	100	100	0.10	0.10
2	110	110	0.09	0.09	110	110	0.09	0.09	110	110	0.09	0.09
3	120	120	0.08	0.08	120	120	0.08	0.08	120	120	0.08	0.08
4	130	130	0.08	0.08	130	130	0.08	0.08	130	130	0.08	0.08
5	140	140	0.07	0.07	140	140	0.07	0.07	140	140	0.07	0.07
6	150	150	0.07	0.07	150	150	0.07	0.07	150	150	0.07	0.07
7	160	160	0.06	0.06	160	160	0.07	0.07	160	160	0.06	0.06
8	170	170	0.06	0.06	170	170	0.06	0.06	170	170	0.06	0.06
9	180	180	0.06	0.06	180	180	0.06	0.06	180	180	0.06	0.06
10	190	190	0.06	0.06	190	190	0.06	0.06	190	190	0.05	0.05
11	200	200	0.05	0.05	200	200	0.05	0.05	200	200	0.05	0.05
12	210	210	0.05	0.05	210	210	0.05	0.05	210	210	0.05	0.05
13	220	220	0.05	0.05	220	220	0.05	0.05	220	220	0.05	0.05
14	230	230	0.05	0.05	230	230	0.05	0.05	230	230	0.05	0.05
15	240	240	0.04	0.04	240	240	0.04	0.04	240	240	0.04	0.04
16	250	250	0.04	0.04	250	250	0.04	0.04	250	250	0.04	0.04
17	260	260	0.04	0.04	260	260	0.04	0.04	260	260	0.04	0.04
18	270	270	0.04	0.04	270	270	0.04	0.04	270	270	0.04	0.04
19	280	280	0.04	0.04	280	280	0.04	0.04	280	280	0.04	0.04
20	290	290	0.04	0.04	290	290	0.04	0.04	290	290	0.04	0.04
21	300	300	0.03	0.03	300	300	0.03	0.03	300	300	0.03	0.03
22	310	310	0.03	0.03	310	310	0.03	0.03	310	310	0.03	0.03
23	320	320	0.03	0.03	320	320	0.03	0.03	320	320	0.03	0.03
24	330	330	0.03	0.03	330	330	0.03	0.03	330	330	0.03	0.03
25	340	220	0.03	-0.33	340	220	0.03	-0.33	340	220	0.03	-0.33
26	350	350	0.03	0.59	350	231	0.03	0.05	350	230	0.03	0.05
27	360	360	0.03	0.03	360	242	0.03	0.05	360	240	0.03	0.04
28	370	370	0.03	0.03	370	253	0.03	0.05	370	250	0.03	0.04
29	380	380	0.03	0.03	380	264	0.03	0.04	380	260	0.03	0.04
30	390	390	0.03	0.03	390	275	0.03	0.04	390	270	0.03	0.04
31	400	400	0.03	0.03	400	286	0.03	0.04	400	280	0.03	0.04
32	410	410	0.03	0.03	410	297	0.03	0.04	410	290	0.03	0.04

33	420	420	0.02	0.02	420	308	0.02	0.04	420	300	0.02	0.03
34	430	430	0.02	0.02	430	319	0.02	0.04	430	310	0.02	0.03
35	440	440	0.02	0.02	440	330	0.02	0.03	440	320	0.02	0.03
36	450	450	0.02	0.02	450	341	0.02	0.03	450	330	0.02	0.03
37	460	460	0.02	0.02	460	352	0.02	0.03	460	340	0.02	0.03
38	470	470	0.02	0.02	470	363	0.02	0.03	470	350	0.02	0.03
39	480	480	0.02	0.02	480	374	0.02	0.03	480	360	0.02	0.03
40	490	490	0.02	0.02	490	385	0.02	0.03	490	370	0.02	0.03
41	500	500	0.02	0.02	500	396	0.02	0.03	500	380	0.02	0.03
42	510	510	0.02	0.02	510	407	0.02	0.03	510	390	0.02	0.03
43	520	520	0.02	0.02	520	418	0.02	0.03	520	400	0.02	0.03
44	530	530	0.02	0.02	530	429	0.02	0.03	530	410	0.02	0.03
45	540	540	0.02	0.02	540	440	0.02	0.03	540	420	0.02	0.02
46	550	550	0.02	0.02	550	451	0.02	0.03	550	430	0.02	0.02
47	560	560	0.02	0.02	560	462	0.02	0.02	560	440	0.02	0.02
48	570	570	0.02	0.02	570	473	0.02	0.02	570	450	0.02	0.02
49	580	580	0.02	0.02	580	484	0.02	0.02	580	460	0.02	0.02
50	590	590	0.02	0.02	590	495	0.02	0.02	590	470	0.02	0.02
51	600	600	0.02	0.02	600	506	0.02	0.02	600	480	0.02	0.02
52	610	610	0.02	0.02	610	517	0.02	0.02	610	490	0.02	0.02
53	620	620	0.02	0.02	620	528	0.02	0.02	620	500	0.02	0.02
54	630	630	0.02	0.02	630	539	0.02	0.02	630	510	0.02	0.02
55	640	640	0.02	0.02	640	550	0.02	0.02	640	520	0.02	0.02
56	650	650	0.02	0.02	650	561	0.02	0.02	650	530	0.02	0.02
57	660	660	0.02	0.02	660	572	0.02	0.02	660	540	0.02	0.02
58	670	670	0.02	0.02	670	583	0.02	0.02	670	550	0.02	0.02
59	680	680	0.01	0.01	680	594	0.02	0.02	680	560	0.02	0.02
60	690	690	0.01	0.01	690	605	0.02	0.02	690	570	0.01	0.02
61	700	700	0.01	0.01	700	616	0.01	0.02	700	580	0.01	0.02
62	710	710	0.01	0.01	710	627	0.01	0.02	710	590	0.01	0.02
63	720	720	0.01	0.01	720	638	0.01	0.02	720	600	0.01	0.02
64	730	730	0.01	0.01	730	649	0.01	0.02	730	610	0.01	0.02
65	740	740	0.01	0.01	740	660	0.01	0.02	740	620	0.01	0.02
66	750	750	0.01	0.01	750	671	0.01	0.02	750	630	0.01	0.02
67	760	760	0.01	0.01	760	682	0.01	0.02	760	640	0.01	0.02
68	770	770	0.01	0.01	770	693	0.01	0.02	770	650	0.01	0.02
69	780	780	0.01	0.01	780	704	0.01	0.02	780	660	0.01	0.02

0.02	0.01	670	790	0.02	0.01	715	790	0.01	0.01	790	790	70
0.01	0.01	680	800	0.02	0.01	726	800	0.01	0.01	800	800	71
0.01	0.01	690	810	0.02	0.01	737	810	0.01	0.01	810	810	72
0.01	0.01	700	820	0.01	0.01	748	820	0.01	0.01	820	820	73
0.01	0.01	710	830	0.01	0.01	759	830	0.01	0.01	830	830	74
0.01	0.01	720	840	0.01	0.01	770	840	0.01	0.01	840	840	75
0.01	0.01	730	850	0.01	0.01	781	850	0.01	0.01	850	850	76
0.01	0.01	740	860	0.01	0.01	792	860	0.01	0.01	860	860	77
0.01	0.01	750	870	0.01	0.01	803	870	0.01	0.01	870	870	78
0.01	0.01	760	880	0.01	0.01	814	880	0.01	0.01	880	880	79
0.01	0.01	770	890	0.01	0.01	825	890	0.01	0.01	890	890	80
0.01	0.01	780	900	0.01	0.01	836	900	0.01	0.01	900	900	81
0.01	0.01	790	910	0.01	0.01	847	910	0.01	0.01	910	910	82
0.01	0.01	800	920	0.01	0.01	858	920	0.01	0.01	920	920	83
0.01	0.01	810	930	0.01	0.01	869	930	0.01	0.01	930	930	84
0.01	0.01	820	940	0.01	0.01	880	940	0.01	0.01	940	940	85
0.01	0.01	830	950	0.01	0.01	891	950	0.01	0.01	950	950	86
0.01	0.01	840	960	0.01	0.01	902	960	0.01	0.01	960	960	87
0.01	0.01	850	970	0.01	0.01	913	970	0.01	0.01	970	970	88
0.01	0.01	860	980	0.01	0.01	924	980	0.01	0.01	980	980	89
0.01	0.01	870	990	0.01	0.01	935	990	0.01	0.01	990	990	90
0.01	0.01	880	1000	0.01	0.01	946	1000	0.01	0.01	1000	1000	91
0.01	0.01	890	1010	0.01	0.01	957	1010	0.01	0.01	1010	1010	92
0.01	0.01	900	1020	0.01	0.01	968	1020	0.01	0.01	1020	1020	93
0.01	0.01	910	1030	0.01	0.01	979	1030	0.01	0.01	1030	1030	94
0.01	0.01	920	1040	0.01	0.01	991	1040	0.01	0.01	1040	1040	95
0.01	0.01	930	1050	0.01	0.01	1003	1050	0.01	0.01	1050	1050	96
0.01	0.01	940	1060	0.01	0.01	1015	1060	0.01	0.01	1060	1060	97
0.01	0.01	950	1070	0.01	0.01	1027	1070	0.01	0.01	1070	1070	98
0.01	0.01	960	1080	0.01	0.01	1039	1080	0.01	0.01	1080	1080	99
0.01	0.01	970	1090	0.01	0.01	1051	1090	0.01	0.01	1090	1090	100
0.01	0.01	980	1100	0.01	0.01	1063	1100	0.01	0.01	1100	1100	101
0.01	0.01	990	1110	0.01	0.01	1075	1110	0.01	0.01	1110	1110	102
0.01	0.01	1000	1120	0.01	0.01	1087	1120	0.01	0.01	1120	1120	103
0.01	0.01	1010	1130	0.01	0.01	1099	1130	0.01	0.01	1130	1130	104
0.01	0.01	1020	1140	0.01	0.01	1111	1140	0.01	0.01	1140	1140	105
0.01	0.01	1030	1150	0.01	0.01	1123	1150	0.01	0.01	1150	1150	106

107	1160	1160	0.01	0.01	1160	1135	0.01	0.01	1160	1040	0.01	0.01
108	1170	1170	0.01	0.01	1170	1147	0.01	0.01	1170	1050	0.01	0.01
109	1180	1180	0.01	0.01	1180	1159	0.01	0.01	1180	1060	0.01	0.01
110	1190	1190	0.01	0.01	1190	1171	0.01	0.01	1190	1070	0.01	0.01
111	1200	1200	0.01	0.01	1200	1183	0.01	0.01	1200	1080	0.01	0.01
112	1210	1210	0.01	0.01	1210	1195	0.01	0.01	1210	1090	0.01	0.01
113	1220	1220	0.01	0.01	1220	1207	0.01	0.01	1220	1100	0.01	0.01
114	1230	1230	0.01	0.01	1230	1219	0.01	0.01	1230	1110	0.01	0.01
115	1240	1240	0.01	0.01	1240	1231	0.01	0.01	1240	1120	0.01	0.01
116	1250	1250	0.01	0.01	1250	1243	0.01	0.01	1250	1130	0.01	0.01
117	1260	1260	0.01	0.01	1260	1255	0.01	0.01	1260	1140	0.01	0.01
118	1270	1270	0.01	0.01	1270	1267	0.01	0.01	1270	1150	0.01	0.01
119	1280	1280	0.01	0.01	1280	1279	0.01	0.01	1280	1160	0.01	0.01
120	1290	1290	0.01	0.01	1290	1290	0.01	0.01	1290	1170	0.01	0.01
corr	1.00		0.30		0.99		0.44		0.99		0.44	

Appendix 8

	Prices (NAV)		Returns		Prices (NAV)		Returns		Prices (NAV)		Returns	
	Cx	Dx	Cx	Dx	Cx'	Dx'	Cx'	Dx'	Cx"	Dx"	Cx"	Dx"
1	100	100	0.10	0.10	100	100	0.10	0.10	100	100	0.10	0.10
2	110	110	0.09	0.09	110	110	0.09	0.09	110	110	0.09	0.09
3	120	120	0.08	0.08	120	120	0.08	0.08	120	120	0.08	0.08
4	130	130	0.08	0.08	130	130	0.08	0.08	130	130	0.08	0.08
5	140	140	0.07	0.07	140	140	0.07	0.07	140	140	0.07	0.07
6	150	150	0.07	0.07	150	150	0.07	0.07	150	150	0.07	0.07
7	160	160	0.06	0.07	160	160	0.07	0.07	160	160	0.07	0.07
8	170	170	0.06	0.06	170	170	0.06	0.06	170	170	0.06	0.06
9	180	180	0.06	0.06	180	180	0.06	0.06	180	180	0.06	0.06
10	190	190	0.06	0.06	190	190	0.06	0.06	190	190	0.06	0.06
11	200	200	0.05	0.05	200	200	0.05	0.05	200	200	0.05	0.05
12	210	210	0.05	0.05	210	210	0.05	0.05	210	210	0.05	0.05
13	220	220	0.05	0.05	220	220	0.05	0.05	220	220	0.05	0.05
14	230	230	0.05	0.05	230	230	0.05	0.05	230	230	0.05	0.05
15	240	240	0.04	0.04	240	240	0.04	0.04	240	240	0.04	0.04
16	250	250	0.04	0.04	250	250	0.04	0.04	250	250	0.04	0.04
17	260	260	0.04	0.04	260	260	0.04	0.04	260	260	0.04	0.04
18	270	270	0.04	0.04	270	270	0.04	0.04	270	270	0.04	0.04
19	280	280	0.04	0.04	280	280	0.04	0.04	280	280	0.04	0.04
20	290	290	0.04	0.04	290	290	0.04	0.04	290	290	0.04	0.04
21	300	300	0.03	0.03	300	300	0.03	0.03	300	300	0.03	0.03
22	310	310	0.03	0.03	310	310	0.03	0.03	310	310	0.03	0.03
23	320	320	0.03	0.03	320	320	0.03	0.03	320	320	0.03	0.03
24	330	330	0.03	0.03	330	330	0.03	0.03	330	330	0.03	0.03
25	340	340	0.03	0.03	340	340	0.03	0.03	340	340	0.03	0.03
26	350	350	0.03	0.03	350	350	0.03	0.03	350	350	0.03	0.03
27	360	360	0.03	0.03	360	360	0.03	0.03	360	360	0.03	0.03
28	370	370	0.03	0.03	370	370	0.03	0.03	370	370	0.03	0.03
29	380	380	0.03	0.03	380	380	0.03	0.03	380	380	0.03	0.03
30	390	390	0.03	0.03	390	390	0.03	0.03	390	390	0.03	0.03
31	400	400	0.03	0.03	400	400	0.03	0.03	400	400	0.03	0.03
32	410	410	0.03	0.03	410	410	0.03	0.03	410	410	0.03	0.03

#												
33	420	420	0.02	0.02	420	420	0.02	0.02	420	420	0.02	0.02
34	430	430	0.02	0.02	430	430	0.02	0.02	430	430	0.02	0.02
35	440	440	0.02	0.02	440	440	0.02	0.02	440	440	0.02	0.02
36	450	450	0.02	0.02	450	450	0.02	0.02	450	450	0.02	0.02
37	460	460	0.02	0.02	460	460	0.02	0.02	460	460	0.02	0.02
38	470	470	0.02	0.02	470	470	0.02	0.02	470	470	0.02	0.02
39	480	480	0.02	0.02	480	480	0.02	0.02	480	480	0.02	0.02
40	490	490	0.02	0.02	490	490	0.02	0.02	490	490	0.02	0.02
41	500	500	0.02	0.02	500	500	0.02	0.02	500	500	0.02	0.02
42	510	510	0.02	0.02	510	510	0.02	0.02	510	510	0.02	0.02
43	520	520	0.02	0.02	520	520	0.02	0.02	520	520	0.02	0.02
44	530	530	0.02	0.02	530	530	0.02	0.02	530	530	0.02	0.02
45	540	540	0.02	0.02	540	540	0.02	0.02	540	540	0.02	0.02
46	550	550	0.02	0.02	550	550	0.02	0.02	550	550	0.02	0.02
47	560	560	0.02	0.02	560	560	0.02	0.02	560	560	0.02	0.02
48	570	570	0.02	0.02	570	570	0.02	0.02	570	570	0.02	0.02
49	580	580	0.02	0.02	580	580	0.02	0.02	580	580	0.02	0.02
50	590	590	0.02	0.02	590	590	0.02	0.02	590	590	0.02	0.02
51	600	600	0.02	0.02	600	600	0.02	0.02	600	600	0.02	0.02
52	610	610	0.02	0.02	610	610	0.02	0.02	610	610	0.02	0.02
53	620	620	0.02	0.02	620	620	0.02	0.02	620	620	0.02	0.02
54	630	630	0.02	0.02	630	630	0.02	0.02	630	630	0.02	0.02
55	640	640	0.02	0.02	640	640	0.02	0.02	640	640	0.02	0.02
56	650	650	0.02	0.02	650	650	0.02	0.02	650	650	0.02	0.02
57	660	660	0.02	0.02	660	660	0.02	0.02	660	660	0.02	0.02
58	670	670	0.02	0.02	670	670	0.02	0.02	670	670	0.02	0.02
59	680	680	0.01	0.01	680	680	0.01	0.01	680	680	0.01	0.01
60	690	690	0.01	0.01	690	690	0.01	0.01	690	690	0.01	0.01
61	700	700	0.01	0.01	700	700	0.01	0.01	700	700	0.01	0.01
62	710	710	0.01	0.01	710	710	0.01	0.01	710	710	0.01	0.01
63	720	720	0.01	0.01	720	720	0.01	0.01	720	720	0.01	0.01
64	730	730	-0.33	0.01	730	730	-0.33	0.01	730	730	-0.33	0.01
65	740	740	0.53	0.01	490	740	0.03	0.01	490	740	0.02	0.01
66	750	750	0.01	0.01	505	750	0.03	0.01	500	750	0.02	0.01
67	760	760	0.01	0.01	520	760	0.03	0.01	510	760	0.02	0.01
68	770	770	0.01	0.01	535	770	0.03	0.01	520	770	0.02	0.01
69	780	780	0.01	0.01	550	780	0.03	0.01	530	780	0.02	0.01

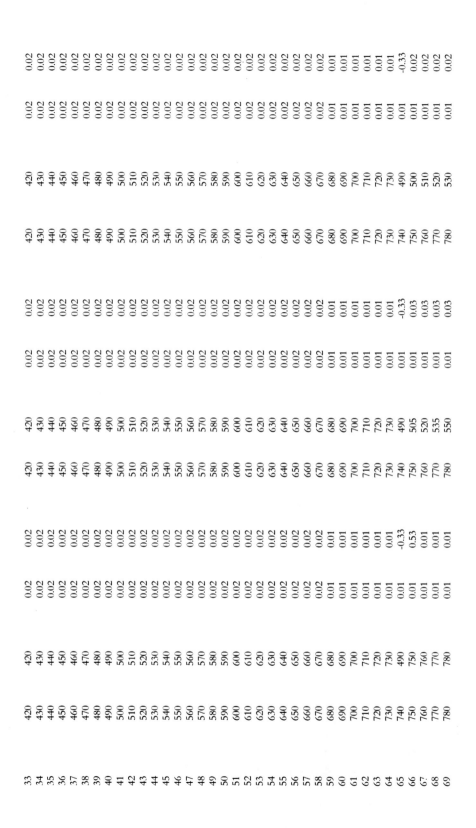

70	790	790	0.01	0.01	790	565	0.01	0.03	790	540	0.01	0.02
71	800	800	0.01	0.01	800	580	0.01	0.03	800	550	0.01	0.02
72	810	810	0.01	0.01	810	595	0.01	0.03	810	560	0.01	0.02
73	820	820	0.01	0.01	820	610	0.01	0.03	820	570	0.01	0.02
74	830	830	0.01	0.01	830	625	0.01	0.02	830	580	0.01	0.02
75	840	840	0.01	0.01	840	640	0.01	0.02	840	590	0.01	0.02
76	850	850	0.01	0.01	850	655	0.01	0.02	850	600	0.01	0.02
77	860	860	0.01	0.01	860	670	0.01	0.02	860	610	0.01	0.02
78	870	870	0.01	0.01	870	685	0.01	0.02	870	620	0.01	0.02
79	880	880	0.01	0.01	880	700	0.01	0.02	880	630	0.01	0.02
80	890	890	0.01	0.01	890	715	0.01	0.02	890	640	0.01	0.02
81	900	900	0.01	0.01	900	730	0.01	0.02	900	650	0.01	0.02
82	910	910	0.01	0.01	910	745	0.01	0.02	910	660	0.01	0.02
83	920	920	0.01	0.01	920	760	0.01	0.02	920	670	0.01	0.01
84	930	930	0.01	0.01	930	775	0.01	0.02	930	680	0.01	0.01
85	940	940	0.01	0.01	940	790	0.01	0.02	940	690	0.01	0.01
86	950	950	0.01	0.01	950	805	0.01	0.02	950	700	0.01	0.01
87	960	960	0.01	0.01	960	820	0.01	0.02	960	710	0.01	0.01
88	970	970	0.01	0.01	970	835	0.01	0.02	970	720	0.01	0.01
89	980	980	0.01	0.01	980	850	0.01	0.02	980	730	0.01	0.01
90	990	990	0.01	0.01	990	865	0.01	0.02	990	740	0.01	0.01
91	1000	1000	0.01	0.01	1000	880	0.01	0.02	1000	750	0.01	0.01
92	1010	1010	0.01	0.01	1010	895	0.01	0.02	1010	760	0.01	0.01
93	1020	1020	0.01	0.01	1020	910	0.01	0.02	1020	770	0.01	0.01
94	1030	1030	0.01	0.01	1030	925	0.01	0.02	1030	780	0.01	0.01
95	1040	1040	0.01	0.01	1040	939	0.01	0.01	1040	790	0.01	0.01
96	1050	1050	0.01	0.01	1050	953	0.01	0.01	1050	800	0.01	0.01
97	1060	1060	0.01	0.01	1060	967	0.01	0.01	1060	810	0.01	0.01
98	1070	1070	0.01	0.01	1070	981	0.01	0.01	1070	820	0.01	0.01
99	1080	1080	0.01	0.01	1080	995	0.01	0.01	1080	830	0.01	0.01
100	1090	1090	0.01	0.01	1090	1009	0.01	0.01	1090	840	0.01	0.01
101	1100	1100	0.01	0.01	1100	1023	0.01	0.01	1100	850	0.01	0.01
102	1110	1110	0.01	0.01	1110	1037	0.01	0.01	1110	860	0.01	0.01
103	1120	1120	0.01	0.01	1120	1051	0.01	0.01	1120	870	0.01	0.01
104	1130	1130	0.01	0.01	1130	1065	0.01	0.01	1130	880	0.01	0.01
105	1140	1140	0.01	0.01	1140	1079	0.01	0.01	1140	890	0.01	0.01
106	1150	1150	0.01	0.01	1150	1093	0.01	0.01	1150	900	0.01	0.01

107	0.01	0.01	910	1160	0.01	1107	1160	0.01	0.01	1160	1160
108	0.01	0.01	920	1170	0.01	1121	1170	0.01	0.01	1170	1170
109	0.01	0.01	930	1180	0.01	1135	1180	0.01	0.01	1180	1180
110	0.01	0.01	940	1190	0.01	1149	1190	0.01	0.01	1190	1190
111	0.01	0.01	950	1200	0.01	1163	1200	0.01	0.01	1200	1200
112	0.01	0.01	960	1210	0.01	1177	1210	0.01	0.01	1210	1210
113	0.01	0.01	970	1220	0.01	1191	1220	0.01	0.01	1220	1220
114	0.01	0.01	980	1230	0.01	1205	1230	0.01	0.01	1230	1230
115	0.01	0.01	990	1240	0.01	1219	1240	0.01	0.01	1240	1240
116	0.01	0.01	1000	1250	0.01	1233	1250	0.01	0.01	1250	1250
117	0.01	0.01	1010	1260	0.01	1247	1260	0.01	0.01	1260	1260
118	0.01	0.01	1020	1270	0.01	1261	1270	0.01	0.01	1270	1270
119	0.01	0.01	1030	1280	0.01	1275	1280	0.01	0.01	1280	1280
120	0.01	0.01	1040	1290	0.01	1290	1290	0.01	0.01	1290	1290
corr	0.51	0.97		0.97	0.48	0.98		0.30		1.00	1.00

Appendix 9

#	Prices (NAV) Ex	Prices (NAV) Ex	Returns Ex	Returns Ex	Prices (NAV) Ex'	Prices (NAV) Ex'	Returns Ex'	Returns Ex'	Prices (NAV) Ex''	Prices (NAV) Ex''	Returns Ex''	Returns Ex''
1	100	100	0.10	0.10	100	100	0.10	0.10	100	100	0.10	0.10
2	110	110	0.09	0.09	110	110	0.09	0.09	110	110	0.09	0.09
3	120	120	0.08	0.08	120	120	0.08	0.08	120	120	0.08	0.08
4	130	130	0.08	0.08	130	130	0.08	0.08	130	130	0.08	0.08
5	140	140	0.07	0.07	140	140	0.07	0.07	140	140	0.07	0.07
6	150	150	0.07	0.07	150	150	0.07	0.07	150	150	0.07	0.07
7	160	160	0.06	0.06	160	160	0.06	0.06	160	160	0.07	0.07
8	170	170	0.06	0.06	170	170	0.06	0.06	170	170	0.06	0.06
9	180	180	0.06	0.06	180	180	0.06	0.06	180	180	0.06	0.06
10	190	190	0.05	0.05	190	190	0.05	0.05	190	190	0.06	0.06
11	200	200	0.05	0.05	200	200	0.05	0.05	200	200	0.05	0.05
12	210	210	0.05	0.05	210	210	0.05	0.05	210	210	0.05	0.05
13	220	220	0.05	0.05	220	220	0.05	0.05	220	220	0.05	0.05
14	230	230	0.04	0.04	230	230	0.04	0.04	230	230	0.05	0.04
15	240	240	0.04	0.04	240	240	0.04	0.04	240	240	0.04	0.04
16	250	250	0.04	0.04	250	250	0.04	0.04	250	250	0.04	0.04
17	260	260	0.04	0.04	260	260	0.04	0.04	260	260	0.04	0.04
18	270	270	0.04	0.04	270	270	0.04	0.04	270	270	0.04	0.04
19	280	280	0.04	0.04	280	280	0.04	0.04	280	280	0.04	0.04
20	290	290	0.04	0.04	290	290	0.04	0.04	290	290	0.04	0.04
21	300	300	0.03	0.03	300	300	0.03	0.03	300	300	0.03	0.03
22	310	310	0.03	0.03	310	310	0.03	0.03	310	310	0.03	0.03
23	320	320	0.03	0.03	320	320	0.03	0.03	320	320	0.03	0.03
24	330	330	0.03	0.03	330	330	0.03	0.03	330	330	0.03	0.03
25	340	340	0.03	0.03	340	340	0.03	0.03	340	340	0.03	0.03
26	350	350	0.03	0.03	350	350	0.03	0.03	350	350	0.03	0.03
27	360	360	0.03	0.03	360	360	0.03	0.03	360	360	0.03	0.03
28	370	370	0.03	0.03	370	370	0.03	0.03	370	370	0.03	0.03
29	380	380	0.03	0.03	380	380	0.03	0.03	380	380	0.03	0.03
30	390	390	0.03	0.03	390	390	0.03	0.03	390	390	0.03	0.03
31	400	400	0.03	0.03	400	400	0.03	0.03	400	400	0.03	0.03
32	410	410	0.03	0.03	410	410	0.03	0.03	410	410	0.03	0.03

33	420	420	0.02	0.02	420	420	0.02	0.02	420	420	0.02	0.02
34	430	430	0.02	0.02	430	430	0.02	0.02	430	430	0.02	0.02
35	440	440	0.02	0.02	440	440	0.02	0.02	440	440	0.02	0.02
36	450	450	0.02	0.02	450	450	0.02	0.02	450	450	0.02	0.02
37	460	460	0.02	0.02	460	460	0.02	0.02	460	460	0.02	0.02
38	470	470	0.02	0.02	470	470	0.02	0.02	470	470	0.02	0.02
39	480	480	0.02	0.02	480	480	0.02	0.02	480	480	0.02	0.02
40	490	490	0.02	0.02	490	490	0.02	0.02	490	490	0.02	0.02
41	500	500	0.02	0.02	500	500	0.02	0.02	500	500	0.02	0.02
42	510	510	0.02	0.02	510	510	0.02	0.02	510	510	0.02	0.02
43	520	520	0.02	0.02	520	520	0.02	0.02	520	520	0.02	0.02
44	530	530	0.02	0.02	530	530	0.02	0.02	530	530	0.02	0.02
45	540	540	0.02	0.02	540	540	0.02	0.02	540	540	0.02	0.02
46	550	550	0.02	0.02	550	550	0.02	0.02	550	550	0.02	0.02
47	560	560	0.02	0.02	560	560	0.02	0.02	560	560	0.02	0.02
48	570	570	0.02	0.02	570	570	0.02	0.02	570	570	0.02	0.02
49	580	580	0.02	0.02	580	580	0.02	0.02	580	580	0.02	0.02
50	590	590	0.02	0.02	590	590	0.02	0.02	590	590	0.02	0.02
51	600	600	0.02	0.02	600	600	0.02	0.02	600	600	0.02	0.02
52	610	610	0.02	0.02	610	610	0.02	0.02	610	610	0.02	0.02
53	620	620	0.02	0.02	620	620	0.02	0.02	620	620	0.02	0.02
54	630	630	0.02	0.02	630	630	0.02	0.02	630	630	0.02	0.02
55	640	640	0.02	0.02	640	640	0.02	0.02	640	640	0.02	0.02
56	650	650	0.02	0.02	650	650	0.02	0.02	650	650	0.02	0.02
57	660	660	0.02	0.02	660	660	0.02	0.02	660	660	0.02	0.02
58	670	670	0.02	0.02	670	670	0.02	0.02	670	670	0.02	0.02
59	680	680	0.02	0.02	680	680	0.02	0.02	680	680	0.02	0.02
60	690	690	0.02	0.02	690	690	0.02	0.02	690	690	0.02	0.02
61	700	700	0.01	0.01	700	700	0.01	0.01	700	700	0.01	0.01
62	710	710	0.01	0.01	710	710	0.01	0.01	710	710	0.01	0.01
63	720	720	0.01	0.01	720	720	0.01	0.01	720	720	0.01	0.01
64	730	730	0.01	0.01	730	730	0.01	0.01	730	730	0.01	0.01
65	740	740	0.01	0.01	740	740	0.01	0.01	740	740	0.01	0.01
66	750	750	0.01	0.01	750	750	0.01	0.01	750	750	0.01	0.01
67	760	760	0.01	0.01	760	760	0.01	0.01	760	760	0.01	0.01
68	770	770	0.01	0.01	770	770	0.01	0.01	770	770	0.01	0.01
69	780	780	0.01	0.01	780	780	0.01	0.01	780	780	0.01	0.01

70	790	790	0.01	0.01	790	790	0.01	0.01	790	790	0.01	0.01
71	800	800	0.01	0.01	800	800	0.01	0.01	800	800	0.01	0.01
72	810	810	0.01	0.01	810	810	0.01	0.01	810	810	0.01	0.01
73	820	820	0.01	0.01	820	820	0.01	0.01	820	820	0.01	0.01
74	830	830	0.01	0.01	830	830	0.01	0.01	830	830	0.01	0.01
75	840	840	0.01	0.01	840	840	0.01	0.01	840	840	0.01	0.01
76	850	850	0.01	0.01	850	850	0.01	0.01	850	850	0.01	0.01
77	860	860	0.01	0.01	860	860	0.01	0.01	860	860	0.01	0.01
78	870	870	0.01	0.01	870	870	0.01	0.01	870	870	0.01	0.01
79	880	880	0.01	0.01	880	880	0.01	0.01	880	880	0.01	0.01
80	890	890	0.01	0.01	890	890	0.01	0.01	890	890	0.01	0.01
81	900	900	0.01	0.01	900	900	0.01	0.01	900	900	0.01	0.01
82	910	910	0.01	0.01	910	910	0.01	0.01	910	910	0.01	0.01
83	920	920	0.01	0.01	920	920	0.01	0.01	920	920	0.01	0.01
84	930	930	0.01	0.01	930	930	0.01	0.01	930	930	0.01	0.01
85	940	940	0.01	0.01	940	940	0.01	0.01	940	940	0.01	0.01
86	950	950	0.01	0.01	950	950	0.01	0.01	950	950	0.01	0.01
87	960	960	0.01	0.01	960	960	0.01	0.01	960	960	0.01	0.01
88	970	970	0.01	0.01	970	970	0.01	0.01	970	970	0.01	0.01
89	980	980	0.01	0.01	980	980	0.01	0.01	980	980	0.01	0.01
90	990	650	0.01	-0.34	990	650	0.01	-0.34	990	650	0.01	-0.34
91	1000	1000	0.01	0.54	1000	670	0.01	0.03	1000	660	0.01	0.02
92	1010	1010	0.01	0.01	1010	691	0.01	0.03	1010	670	0.01	0.02
93	1020	1020	0.01	0.01	1020	712	0.01	0.03	1020	680	0.01	0.01
94	1030	1030	0.01	0.01	1030	733	0.01	0.03	1030	690	0.01	0.01
95	1040	1040	0.01	0.01	1040	754	0.01	0.03	1040	700	0.01	0.01
96	1050	1050	0.01	0.01	1050	775	0.01	0.03	1050	710	0.01	0.01
97	1060	1060	0.01	0.01	1060	796	0.01	0.03	1060	720	0.01	0.01
98	1070	1070	0.01	0.01	1070	817	0.01	0.03	1070	730	0.01	0.01
99	1080	1080	0.01	0.01	1080	838	0.01	0.03	1080	740	0.01	0.01
100	1090	1090	0.01	0.01	1090	859	0.01	0.03	1090	750	0.01	0.01
101	1100	1100	0.01	0.01	1100	880	0.01	0.02	1100	760	0.01	0.01
102	1110	1110	0.01	0.01	1110	901	0.01	0.02	1110	770	0.01	0.01
103	1120	1120	0.01	0.01	1120	922	0.01	0.02	1120	780	0.01	0.01
104	1130	1130	0.01	0.01	1130	943	0.01	0.02	1130	790	0.01	0.01
105	1140	1140	0.01	0.01	1140	964	0.01	0.02	1140	800	0.01	0.01
106	1150	1150	0.01	0.01	1150	985	0.01	0.02	1150	810	0.01	0.01

107	1160	1160	0.01	0.01	1160	1006	0.01	0.02	1160	820	0.01	0.01
108	1170	1170	0.01	0.01	1170	1027	0.01	0.02	1170	830	0.01	0.01
109	1180	1180	0.01	0.01	1180	1049	0.01	0.02	1180	840	0.01	0.01
110	1190	1190	0.01	0.01	1190	1071	0.01	0.02	1190	850	0.01	0.01
111	1200	1200	0.01	0.01	1200	1093	0.01	0.02	1200	860	0.01	0.01
112	1210	1210	0.01	0.01	1210	1115	0.01	0.02	1210	870	0.01	0.01
113	1220	1220	0.01	0.01	1220	1137	0.01	0.02	1220	880	0.01	0.01
114	1230	1230	0.01	0.01	1230	1159	0.01	0.02	1230	890	0.01	0.01
115	1240	1240	0.01	0.01	1240	1181	0.01	0.02	1240	900	0.01	0.01
116	1250	1250	0.01	0.01	1250	1203	0.01	0.02	1250	910	0.01	0.01
117	1260	1260	0.01	0.01	1260	1225	0.01	0.02	1260	920	0.01	0.01
118	1270	1270	0.01	0.01	1270	1247	0.01	0.02	1270	930	0.01	0.01
119	1280	1280	0.01	0.01	1280	1269	0.01	0.02	1280	940	0.01	0.01
120	1290	1290	0.01	0.01	1290	1290	0.01	0.02	1290	950	0.01	0.01
corr	1.00		0.29		0.97		0.48		0.92		0.52	

Appendix 10

	Prices (NAV)		Returns		Prices (NAV)		Returns		Prices (NAV)		Returns	
	Xs	Ys	Xs	Ys	Xs'	Ys'	Xs'	Ys'	Xs"	Ys"	Xs"	Ys"
1	100	100			100	100			100	100		
2	105	105	0.05	0.05	105	105	0.05	0.05	105	105	0.05	0.05
3	110	110	0.05	0.05	110	110	0.05	0.05	110	110	0.05	0.05
4	116	116	0.05	0.05	116	116	0.05	0.05	116	116	0.05	0.05
5	122	122	0.05	0.05	122	122	0.05	0.05	122	122	0.05	0.05
6	128	128	0.05	0.05	128	128	0.05	0.05	128	128	0.05	0.05
7	134	134	0.05	0.05	134	134	0.05	0.05	134	134	0.05	0.05
8	141	141	0.05	0.05	141	141	0.05	0.05	141	141	0.05	0.05
9	148	148	0.05	0.05	148	148	0.05	0.05	148	148	0.05	0.05
10	155	155	0.05	0.05	155	155	0.05	0.05	155	155	0.05	0.05
11	163	163	0.05	0.05	163	163	0.05	0.05	163	163	0.05	0.05
12	171	171	0.05	0.05	171	171	0.05	0.05	171	171	0.05	0.05
13	180	180	0.05	0.05	180	180	0.05	0.05	180	180	0.05	0.05
14	189	189	0.05	0.05	189	189	0.05	0.05	189	189	0.05	0.05
15	198	198	0.05	0.05	198	198	0.05	0.05	198	198	0.05	0.05
16	208	208	0.05	0.05	208	208	0.05	0.05	208	208	0.05	0.05
17	218	218	0.05	0.05	218	218	0.05	0.05	218	218	0.05	0.05
18	229	229	0.05	0.05	229	229	0.05	0.05	229	229	0.05	0.05
19	241	241	0.05	0.05	241	241	0.05	0.05	241	241	0.05	0.05
20	253	253	0.05	0.05	253	253	0.05	0.05	253	253	0.05	0.05
21	265	265	0.05	0.05	265	265	0.05	0.05	265	265	0.05	0.05
22	279	279	0.05	0.05	279	279	0.05	0.05	279	279	0.05	0.05
23	293	293	0.05	0.05	293	293	0.05	0.05	293	293	0.05	0.05
24	307	307	0.05	0.05	307	307	0.05	0.05	307	307	0.05	0.05
25	323	205	0.05	-0.33	323	205	0.05	-0.33	323	205	0.05	-0.33
26	339	339	0.05	0.65	339	216	0.05	0.06	339	215	0.05	0.05
27	356	356	0.05	0.05	356	228	0.05	0.06	356	226	0.05	0.05
28	373	373	0.05	0.05	373	241	0.05	0.06	373	237	0.05	0.05
29	392	392	0.05	0.05	392	254	0.05	0.06	392	249	0.05	0.05
30	412	412	0.05	0.05	412	268	0.05	0.06	412	262	0.05	0.05
31	432	432	0.05	0.05	432	283	0.05	0.06	432	275	0.05	0.05
32	454	454	0.05	0.05	454	298	0.05	0.06	454	288	0.05	0.05

33	476	476	0.05	0.05	315	476	0.05	0.06	476	303	0.05	0.05
34	500	500	0.05	0.05	332	500	0.05	0.06	500	318	0.05	0.05
35	525	525	0.05	0.05	350	525	0.05	0.06	525	334	0.05	0.05
36	552	552	0.05	0.05	369	552	0.05	0.06	552	351	0.05	0.05
37	579	579	0.05	0.05	390	579	0.05	0.06	579	368	0.05	0.05
38	608	608	0.05	0.05	411	608	0.05	0.05	608	387	0.05	0.05
39	639	639	0.05	0.05	434	639	0.05	0.06	639	406	0.05	0.05
40	670	670	0.05	0.05	458	670	0.05	0.06	670	426	0.05	0.05
41	704	704	0.05	0.05	483	704	0.05	0.06	704	447	0.05	0.05
42	739	739	0.05	0.05	509	739	0.05	0.06	739	470	0.05	0.05
43	776	776	0.05	0.05	537	776	0.05	0.06	776	493	0.05	0.05
44	815	815	0.05	0.05	567	815	0.05	0.06	815	518	0.05	0.05
45	856	856	0.05	0.05	598	856	0.05	0.06	856	544	0.05	0.05
46	899	899	0.05	0.05	631	899	0.05	0.06	899	571	0.05	0.05
47	943	943	0.05	0.05	666	943	0.05	0.05	943	600	0.05	0.05
48	991	991	0.05	0.05	702	991	0.05	0.06	991	630	0.05	0.05
49	1040	1040	0.05	0.05	741	1040	0.05	0.06	1040	661	0.05	0.05
50	1092	1092	0.05	0.05	782	1092	0.05	0.06	1092	694	0.05	0.05
51	1147	1147	0.05	0.05	825	1147	0.05	0.06	1147	729	0.05	0.05
52	1204	1204	0.05	0.05	870	1204	0.05	0.06	1204	765	0.05	0.05
53	1264	1264	0.05	0.05	918	1264	0.05	0.06	1264	804	0.05	0.05
54	1327	1327	0.05	0.05	968	1327	0.05	0.06	1327	844	0.05	0.05
55	1394	1394	0.05	0.05	1022	1394	0.05	0.06	1394	886	0.05	0.05
56	1464	1464	0.05	0.05	1078	1464	0.05	0.05	1464	930	0.05	0.05
57	1537	1537	0.05	0.05	1137	1537	0.05	0.05	1537	977	0.05	0.05
58	1614	1614	0.05	0.05	1200	1614	0.05	0.05	1614	1026	0.05	0.05
59	1694	1694	0.05	0.05	1266	1694	0.05	0.06	1694	1077	0.05	0.05
60	1779	1779	0.05	0.05	1335	1779	0.05	0.06	1779	1131	0.05	0.05
61	1868	1868	0.05	0.05	1409	1868	0.05	0.05	1868	1187	0.05	0.05
62	1961	1961	0.05	0.05	1486	1961	0.05	0.06	1961	1247	0.05	0.05
63	2059	2059	0.05	0.05	1568	2059	0.05	0.06	2059	1309	0.05	0.05
64	2162	2162	0.05	0.05	1654	2162	0.05	0.06	2162	1374	0.05	0.05
65	2270	2270	0.05	0.05	1745	2270	0.05	0.06	2270	1443	0.05	0.05
66	2384	2384	0.05	0.05	1841	2384	0.05	0.06	2384	1515	0.05	0.05
67	2503	2503	0.05	0.05	1942	2503	0.05	0.06	2503	1591	0.05	0.05
68	2628	2628	0.05	0.05	2049	2628	0.05	0.05	2628	1671	0.05	0.05
69	2760	2760	0.05	0.05	2162	2760	0.05	0.06	2760	1754	0.05	0.05

0.05	0.05	1842	2898	0.06	0.05	2281	2898	0.05	0.05	2898	2898	70
0.05	0.05	1934	3043	0.06	0.05	2406	3043	0.05	0.05	3043	3043	71
0.05	0.05	2031	3195	0.06	0.05	2539	3195	0.05	0.05	3195	3195	72
0.05	0.05	2132	3355	0.06	0.05	2678	3355	0.05	0.05	3355	3355	73
0.05	0.05	2239	3522	0.06	0.05	2826	3522	0.05	0.05	3522	3522	74
0.05	0.05	2351	3698	0.06	0.05	2981	3698	0.05	0.05	3698	3698	75
0.05	0.05	2468	3883	0.06	0.05	3145	3883	0.05	0.05	3883	3883	76
0.05	0.05	2592	4077	0.06	0.05	3318	4077	0.05	0.05	4077	4077	77
0.05	0.05	2721	4281	0.06	0.05	3501	4281	0.05	0.05	4281	4281	78
0.05	0.05	2857	4495	0.06	0.05	3693	4495	0.05	0.05	4495	4495	79
0.05	0.05	3000	4720	0.06	0.05	3896	4720	0.05	0.05	4720	4720	80
0.05	0.05	3150	4956	0.06	0.05	4110	4956	0.05	0.05	4956	4956	81
0.05	0.05	3308	5204	0.05	0.05	4337	5204	0.05	0.05	5204	5204	82
0.05	0.05	3473	5464	0.05	0.05	4575	5464	0.05	0.05	5464	5464	83
0.05	0.05	3647	5737	0.06	0.05	4827	5737	0.05	0.05	5737	5737	84
0.05	0.05	3829	6024	0.06	0.05	5092	6024	0.05	0.05	6024	6024	85
0.05	0.05	4021	6325	0.05	0.05	5372	6325	0.05	0.05	6325	6325	86
0.05	0.05	4222	6642	0.06	0.05	5668	6642	0.05	0.05	6642	6642	87
0.05	0.05	4433	6974	0.05	0.05	5979	6974	0.05	0.05	6974	6974	88
0.05	0.05	4654	7322	0.06	0.05	6308	7322	0.05	0.05	7322	7322	89
0.05	0.05	4887	7689	0.05	0.05	6655	7689	0.05	0.05	7689	7689	90
0.05	0.05	5132	8073	0.05	0.05	7021	8073	0.05	0.05	8073	8073	91
0.05	0.05	5388	8477	0.06	0.05	7407	8477	0.05	0.05	8477	8477	92
0.05	0.05	5658	8901	0.06	0.05	7815	8901	0.05	0.05	8901	8901	93
0.05	0.05	5940	9346	0.05	0.05	8245	9346	0.05	0.05	9346	9346	94
0.05	0.05	6237	9813	0.05	0.05	8698	9813	0.05	0.05	9813	9813	95
0.05	0.05	6549	10303	0.06	0.05	9177	10303	0.05	0.05	10303	10303	96
0.05	0.05	6877	10819	0.06	0.05	9681	10819	0.05	0.05	10819	10819	97
0.05	0.05	7221	11360	0.05	0.05	10214	11360	0.05	0.05	11360	11360	98
0.05	0.05	7582	11928	0.06	0.05	10775	11928	0.05	0.05	11928	11928	99
0.05	0.05	7961	12524	0.06	0.05	11368	12524	0.05	0.05	12524	12524	100
0.05	0.05	8359	13150	0.05	0.05	11993	13150	0.05	0.05	13150	13150	101
0.05	0.05	8777	13808	0.06	0.05	12653	13808	0.05	0.05	13808	13808	102
0.05	0.05	9216	14498	0.06	0.05	13349	14498	0.05	0.05	14498	14498	103
0.05	0.05	9676	15223	0.06	0.05	14083	15223	0.05	0.05	15223	15223	104
0.05	0.05	10160	15984	0.05	0.05	14858	15984	0.05	0.05	15984	15984	105
0.05	0.05	10668	16783	0.06	0.05	15675	16783	0.05	0.05	16783	16783	106

107	17622	17622	0.05	0.05	17622	16537	0.05	0.06	17622	11202	0.05	0.05
108	18504	18504	0.05	0.05	18504	17446	0.05	0.06	18504	11762	0.05	0.05
109	19429	19429	0.05	0.05	19429	18410	0.05	0.06	19429	12350	0.05	0.05
110	20400	20400	0.05	0.05	20400	19427	0.05	0.06	20400	12967	0.05	0.05
111	21420	21420	0.05	0.05	21420	20499	0.05	0.06	21420	13615	0.05	0.05
112	22491	22491	0.05	0.05	22491	21631	0.05	0.06	22491	14296	0.05	0.05
113	23616	23616	0.05	0.05	23616	22824	0.05	0.06	23616	15011	0.05	0.05
114	24797	24797	0.05	0.05	24797	24084	0.05	0.06	24797	15762	0.05	0.05
115	26036	26036	0.05	0.05	26036	25412	0.05	0.06	26036	16550	0.05	0.05
116	27338	27338	0.05	0.05	27338	26813	0.05	0.06	27338	17377	0.05	0.05
117	28705	28705	0.05	0.05	28705	28290	0.05	0.06	28705	18246	0.05	0.05
118	30140	30140	0.05	0.05	30140	29849	0.05	0.06	30140	19158	0.05	0.05
119	31647	31647	0.05	0.05	31647	31494	0.05	0.06	31647	20116	0.05	0.05
120	33230	33230	0.05	0.05	33230	33230	0.05	0.06	33230	21122	0.05	0.05
corr	1.00		0.08		1.00		0.08		1.00		0.08	

Appendix 11

	Prices (NAV) Yx	Prices (NAV) Wx	Returns Yx	Returns Wx	Prices (NAV) Yx'	Prices (NAV) Wx'	Returns Yx'	Returns Wx'	Prices (NAV) Yx"	Prices (NAV) Wx"	Returns Yx"	Returns Wx"
1	100	100			100	100			100	100		
2	105	105	0.05	0.05	105	105	0.05	0.05	105	105	0.05	0.05
3	110	110	0.05	0.05	110	110	0.05	0.05	110	110	0.05	0.05
4	116	116	0.05	0.05	116	116	0.05	0.05	116	116	0.05	0.05
5	122	122	0.05	0.05	122	122	0.05	0.05	122	122	0.05	0.05
6	128	128	0.05	0.05	128	128	0.05	0.05	128	128	0.05	0.05
7	134	134	0.05	0.05	134	134	0.05	0.05	134	134	0.05	0.05
8	141	141	0.05	0.05	141	141	0.05	0.05	141	141	0.05	0.05
9	148	148	0.05	0.05	148	148	0.05	0.05	148	148	0.05	0.05
10	155	155	0.05	0.05	155	155	0.05	0.05	155	155	0.05	0.05
11	163	163	0.05	0.05	163	163	0.05	0.05	163	163	0.05	0.05
12	171	171	0.05	0.05	171	171	0.05	0.05	171	171	0.05	0.05
13	180	180	0.05	0.05	180	180	0.05	0.05	180	180	0.05	0.05
14	189	189	0.05	0.05	189	189	0.05	0.05	189	189	0.05	0.05
15	198	198	0.05	0.05	198	198	0.05	0.05	198	198	0.05	0.05
16	208	208	0.05	0.05	208	208	0.05	0.05	208	208	0.05	0.05
17	218	218	0.05	0.05	218	218	0.05	0.05	218	218	0.05	0.05
18	229	229	0.05	0.05	229	229	0.05	0.05	229	229	0.05	0.05
19	241	241	0.05	0.05	241	241	0.05	0.05	241	241	0.05	0.05
20	253	253	0.05	0.05	253	253	0.05	0.05	253	253	0.05	0.05
21	265	265	0.05	0.05	265	265	0.05	0.05	265	265	0.05	0.05
22	279	279	0.05	0.05	279	279	0.05	0.05	279	279	0.05	0.05
23	293	293	0.05	0.05	293	293	0.05	0.05	293	293	0.05	0.05
24	307	307	0.05	0.05	307	307	0.05	0.05	307	307	0.05	0.05
25	323	323	0.05	0.05	323	323	0.05	0.05	323	323	0.05	0.05
26	339	339	0.05	0.05	339	339	0.05	0.05	339	339	0.05	0.05
27	356	356	0.05	0.05	356	356	0.05	0.05	356	356	0.05	0.05
28	373	373	0.05	0.05	373	373	0.05	0.05	373	373	0.05	0.05
29	392	392	0.05	0.05	392	392	0.05	0.05	392	392	0.05	0.05
30	412	412	0.05	0.05	412	412	0.05	0.05	412	412	0.05	0.05
31	432	432	0.05	0.05	432	432	0.05	0.05	432	432	0.05	0.05
32	454	454	0.05	0.05	454	454	0.05	0.05	454	454	0.05	0.05

33	476	476	0.05	0.05	476	476	0.05	0.05	476	476	0.05	0.05
34	500	500	0.05	0.05	500	500	0.05	0.05	500	500	0.05	0.05
35	525	525	0.05	0.05	525	525	0.05	0.05	525	525	0.05	0.05
36	552	552	0.05	0.05	552	552	0.05	0.05	552	552	0.05	0.05
37	579	579	0.05	0.05	579	579	0.05	0.05	579	579	0.05	0.05
38	608	608	0.05	0.05	608	608	0.05	0.05	608	608	0.05	0.05
39	639	639	0.05	0.05	639	639	0.05	0.05	639	639	0.05	0.05
40	670	670	0.05	0.05	670	670	0.05	0.05	670	670	0.05	0.05
41	704	704	0.05	0.05	704	704	0.05	0.05	704	704	0.05	0.05
42	739	739	0.05	0.05	739	739	0.05	0.05	739	739	0.05	0.05
43	776	776	0.05	0.05	776	776	0.05	0.05	776	776	0.05	0.05
44	815	815	0.05	0.05	815	815	0.05	0.05	815	815	0.05	0.05
45	856	856	0.05	0.05	856	856	0.05	0.05	856	856	0.05	0.05
46	899	899	0.05	0.05	899	899	0.05	0.05	899	899	0.05	0.05
47	943	943	0.05	0.05	943	943	0.05	0.05	943	943	0.05	0.05
48	991	991	0.05	0.05	991	991	0.05	0.05	991	991	0.05	0.05
49	1040	1040	0.05	0.05	1040	1040	0.05	0.05	1040	1040	0.05	0.05
50	1092	1092	0.05	0.05	1092	1092	0.05	0.05	1092	1092	0.05	0.05
51	1147	1147	0.05	0.05	1147	1147	0.05	0.05	1147	1147	0.05	0.05
52	1204	1204	0.05	0.05	1204	1204	0.05	0.05	1204	1204	0.05	0.05
53	1264	1264	0.05	0.05	1264	1264	0.05	0.05	1264	1264	0.05	0.05
54	1327	1327	0.05	0.05	1327	1327	0.05	0.05	1327	1327	0.05	0.05
55	1394	1394	0.05	0.05	1394	1394	0.05	0.05	1394	1394	0.05	0.05
56	1464	1464	0.05	0.05	1464	1464	0.05	0.05	1464	1464	0.05	0.05
57	1537	1537	0.05	0.05	1537	1537	0.05	0.05	1537	1537	0.05	0.05
58	1614	1614	0.05	0.05	1614	1614	0.05	0.05	1614	1614	0.05	0.05
59	1694	1694	0.05	0.05	1694	1694	0.05	0.05	1694	1694	0.05	0.05
60	1779	1779	0.05	0.05	1779	1779	0.05	0.05	1779	1779	0.05	0.05
61	1868	1868	0.05	0.05	1868	1868	0.05	0.05	1868	1868	0.05	0.05
62	1961	1961	0.05	0.05	1961	1961	0.05	0.05	1961	1961	0.05	0.05
63	2059	2059	0.05	0.05	2059	2059	0.05	0.05	2059	2059	0.05	0.05
64	2162	2162	0.05	0.05	2162	2162	0.05	0.05	2162	2162	0.05	0.05
65	1462	2270	0.05	-0.32	1462	2270	0.05	-0.32	1462	2270	0.05	-0.32
66	2384	2384	0.05	0.63	1548	2384	0.05	0.06	1535	2384	0.05	0.05
67	2503	2503	0.05	0.05	1638	2503	0.05	0.06	1612	2503	0.05	0.05
68	2628	2628	0.05	0.05	1734	2628	0.05	0.06	1692	2628	0.05	0.05
69	2760	2760	0.05	0.05	1835	2760	0.05	0.06	1777	2760	0.05	0.05

70	2898	2898	0.05	0.05	2898	1943	0.05	0.06	2898	1866	0.05	0.05
71	3043	3043	0.05	0.05	3043	2056	0.05	0.06	3043	1959	0.05	0.05
72	3195	3195	0.05	0.05	3195	2177	0.05	0.06	3195	2057	0.05	0.05
73	3355	3355	0.05	0.05	3355	2304	0.05	0.06	3355	2160	0.05	0.05
74	3522	3522	0.05	0.05	3522	2439	0.05	0.06	3522	2268	0.05	0.05
75	3698	3698	0.05	0.05	3698	2581	0.05	0.06	3698	2381	0.05	0.05
76	3883	3883	0.05	0.05	3883	2732	0.05	0.06	3883	2501	0.05	0.05
77	4077	4077	0.05	0.05	4077	2892	0.05	0.06	4077	2626	0.05	0.05
78	4281	4281	0.05	0.05	4281	3061	0.05	0.06	4281	2757	0.05	0.05
79	4495	4495	0.05	0.05	4495	3241	0.05	0.06	4495	2895	0.05	0.05
80	4720	4720	0.05	0.05	4720	3430	0.05	0.06	4720	3039	0.05	0.05
81	4956	4956	0.05	0.05	4956	3631	0.05	0.06	4956	3191	0.05	0.05
82	5204	5204	0.05	0.05	5204	3843	0.05	0.06	5204	3351	0.05	0.05
83	5464	5464	0.05	0.05	5464	4068	0.05	0.06	5464	3518	0.05	0.05
84	5737	5737	0.05	0.05	5737	4306	0.05	0.06	5737	3694	0.05	0.05
85	6024	6024	0.05	0.05	6024	4558	0.05	0.06	6024	3879	0.05	0.05
86	6325	6325	0.05	0.05	6325	4825	0.05	0.06	6325	4073	0.05	0.05
87	6642	6642	0.05	0.05	6642	5107	0.05	0.06	6642	4277	0.05	0.05
88	6974	6974	0.05	0.05	6974	5406	0.05	0.06	6974	4491	0.05	0.05
89	7322	7323	0.05	0.05	7322	5722	0.05	0.06	7322	4715	0.05	0.05
90	7689	7689	0.05	0.05	7689	6056	0.05	0.06	7689	4951	0.05	0.05
91	8073	8073	0.05	0.05	8073	6411	0.05	0.06	8073	5198	0.05	0.05
92	8477	8477	0.05	0.05	8477	6786	0.05	0.06	8477	5458	0.05	0.05
93	8901	8901	0.05	0.05	8901	7183	0.05	0.06	8901	5731	0.05	0.05
94	9346	9346	0.05	0.05	9346	7603	0.05	0.06	9346	6018	0.05	0.05
95	9813	9813	0.05	0.05	9813	8048	0.05	0.06	9813	6319	0.05	0.05
96	10303	10304	0.05	0.05	10303	8519	0.05	0.06	10303	6635	0.05	0.05
97	10819	10819	0.05	0.05	10819	9017	0.05	0.06	10819	6966	0.05	0.05
98	11360	11360	0.05	0.05	11360	9544	0.05	0.06	11360	7315	0.05	0.05
99	11928	11928	0.05	0.05	11928	10103	0.05	0.06	11928	7680	0.05	0.05
100	12524	12524	0.05	0.05	12524	10694	0.05	0.06	12524	8064	0.05	0.05
101	13150	13150	0.05	0.05	13150	11319	0.05	0.06	13150	8468	0.05	0.05
102	13808	13808	0.05	0.05	13808	11981	0.05	0.06	13808	8891	0.05	0.05
103	14498	14498	0.05	0.05	14498	12682	0.05	0.06	14498	9336	0.05	0.05
104	15223	15223	0.05	0.05	15223	13424	0.05	0.06	15223	9802	0.05	0.05
105	15984	15984	0.05	0.05	15984	14210	0.05	0.06	15984	10292	0.05	0.05
106	16783	16783	0.05	0.05	16783	15041	0.05	0.06	16783	10807	0.05	0.05

107	17622	17622	0.05	0.05	15921	17622	0.05	0.06	11347	17622	0.05	0.05
108	18504	18504	0.05	0.05	16852	18504	0.05	0.06	11915	18504	0.05	0.05
109	19429	19429	0.05	0.05	17838	19429	0.05	0.06	12511	19429	0.05	0.05
110	20400	20400	0.05	0.05	18874	20400	0.05	0.06	13136	20400	0.05	0.05
111	21420	21420	0.05	0.05	19972	21420	0.05	0.06	13793	21420	0.05	0.05
112	22491	22491	0.05	0.05	21133	22491	0.05	0.06	14483	22491	0.05	0.05
113	23616	23616	0.05	0.05	22362	23616	0.05	0.06	15207	23616	0.05	0.05
114	24797	24797	0.05	0.05	23663	24797	0.05	0.06	15967	24797	0.05	0.05
115	26036	26036	0.05	0.05	25041	26036	0.05	0.06	16765	26036	0.05	0.05
116	27338	27338	0.05	0.05	26499	27338	0.05	0.06	17604	27338	0.05	0.05
117	28705	28705	0.05	0.05	28041	28705	0.05	0.06	18484	28705	0.05	0.05
118	30140	30140	0.05	0.05	29673	30140	0.05	0.06	19408	30140	0.05	0.05
119	31647	31647	0.05	0.05	31401	31647	0.05	0.06	20378	31647	0.05	0.05
120	33230	33230	0.05	0.05	33230	33230	0.05	0.06	21397	33230	0.05	0.05
corr	1.00			-0.08	1.00			-0.05	1.00			-0.06

Appendix 12

#	Prices (NAV) Tx	Ux	Returns Tx	Ux	Prices (NAV) Tx'	Ux'	Returns Tx'	Ux'	Prices (NAV) Tx"	Ux"	Returns Tx"	Ux"
1	100	100	0.05	0.05	100	100	0.05	0.05	100	100	0.05	0.05
2	105	105	0.05	0.05	105	105	0.05	0.05	105	105	0.05	0.05
3	110	110	0.05	0.05	110	110	0.05	0.05	110	110	0.05	0.05
4	116	116	0.05	0.05	116	116	0.05	0.05	116	116	0.05	0.05
5	122	122	0.05	0.05	122	122	0.05	0.05	122	122	0.05	0.05
6	128	128	0.05	0.05	128	128	0.05	0.05	128	128	0.05	0.05
7	134	134	0.05	0.05	134	134	0.05	0.05	134	134	0.05	0.05
8	141	141	0.05	0.05	141	141	0.05	0.05	141	141	0.05	0.05
9	148	148	0.05	0.05	148	148	0.05	0.05	148	148	0.05	0.05
10	155	155	0.05	0.05	155	155	0.05	0.05	155	155	0.05	0.05
11	163	163	0.05	0.05	163	163	0.05	0.05	163	163	0.05	0.05
12	171	171	0.05	0.05	171	171	0.05	0.05	171	171	0.05	0.05
13	180	180	0.05	0.05	180	180	0.05	0.05	180	180	0.05	0.05
14	189	189	0.05	0.05	189	189	0.05	0.05	189	189	0.05	0.05
15	198	198	0.05	0.05	198	198	0.05	0.05	198	198	0.05	0.05
16	208	208	0.05	0.05	208	208	0.05	0.05	208	208	0.05	0.05
17	218	218	0.05	0.05	218	218	0.05	0.05	218	218	0.05	0.05
18	229	229	0.05	0.05	229	229	0.05	0.05	229	229	0.05	0.05
19	241	241	0.05	0.05	241	241	0.05	0.05	241	241	0.05	0.05
20	253	253	0.05	0.05	253	253	0.05	0.05	253	253	0.05	0.05
21	265	265	0.05	0.05	265	265	0.05	0.05	265	265	0.05	0.05
22	279	279	0.05	0.05	279	279	0.05	0.05	279	279	0.05	0.05
23	293	293	0.05	0.05	293	293	0.05	0.05	293	293	0.05	0.05
24	307	307	0.05	0.05	307	307	0.05	0.05	307	307	0.05	0.05
25	323	323	0.05	0.05	323	323	0.05	0.05	323	323	0.05	0.05
26	339	339	0.05	0.05	339	339	0.05	0.05	339	339	0.05	0.05
27	356	356	0.05	0.05	356	356	0.05	0.05	356	356	0.05	0.05
28	373	373	0.05	0.05	373	373	0.05	0.05	373	373	0.05	0.05
29	392	392	0.05	0.05	392	392	0.05	0.05	392	392	0.05	0.05
30	412	412	0.05	0.05	412	412	0.05	0.05	412	412	0.05	0.05
31	432	432	0.05	0.05	432	432	0.05	0.05	432	432	0.05	0.05
32	454	454	0.05	0.05	454	454	0.05	0.05	454	454	0.05	0.05

33	476	476	0.05	0.05	476	476	0.05	0.05	476	476	0.05	0.05
34	500	500	0.05	0.05	500	500	0.05	0.05	500	500	0.05	0.05
35	525	525	0.05	0.05	525	525	0.05	0.05	525	525	0.05	0.05
36	552	552	0.05	0.05	552	552	0.05	0.05	552	552	0.05	0.05
37	579	579	0.05	0.05	579	579	0.05	0.05	579	579	0.05	0.05
38	608	608	0.05	0.05	608	608	0.05	0.05	608	608	0.05	0.05
39	639	639	0.05	0.05	639	639	0.05	0.05	639	639	0.05	0.05
40	670	670	0.05	0.05	670	670	0.05	0.05	670	670	0.05	0.05
41	704	704	0.05	0.05	704	704	0.05	0.05	704	704	0.05	0.05
42	739	739	0.05	0.05	739	739	0.05	0.05	739	739	0.05	0.05
43	776	776	0.05	0.05	776	776	0.05	0.05	776	776	0.05	0.05
44	815	815	0.05	0.05	815	815	0.05	0.05	815	815	0.05	0.05
45	856	856	0.05	0.05	856	856	0.05	0.05	856	856	0.05	0.05
46	899	899	0.05	0.05	899	899	0.05	0.05	899	899	0.05	0.05
47	943	943	0.05	0.05	943	943	0.05	0.05	943	943	0.05	0.05
48	991	991	0.05	0.05	991	991	0.05	0.05	991	991	0.05	0.05
49	1040	1040	0.05	0.05	1040	1040	0.05	0.05	1040	1040	0.05	0.05
50	1092	1092	0.05	0.05	1092	1092	0.05	0.05	1092	1092	0.05	0.05
51	1147	1147	0.05	0.05	1147	1147	0.05	0.05	1147	1147	0.05	0.05
52	1204	1204	0.05	0.05	1204	1204	0.05	0.05	1204	1204	0.05	0.05
53	1264	1264	0.05	0.05	1264	1264	0.05	0.05	1264	1264	0.05	0.05
54	1327	1327	0.05	0.05	1327	1327	0.05	0.05	1327	1327	0.05	0.05
55	1394	1394	0.05	0.05	1394	1394	0.05	0.05	1394	1394	0.05	0.05
56	1464	1464	0.05	0.05	1464	1464	0.05	0.05	1464	1464	0.05	0.05
57	1537	1537	0.05	0.05	1537	1537	0.05	0.05	1537	1537	0.05	0.05
58	1614	1614	0.05	0.05	1614	1614	0.05	0.05	1614	1614	0.05	0.05
59	1694	1694	0.05	0.05	1694	1694	0.05	0.05	1694	1694	0.05	0.05
60	1779	1779	0.05	0.05	1779	1779	0.05	0.05	1779	1779	0.05	0.05
61	1868	1868	0.05	0.05	1868	1868	0.05	0.05	1868	1868	0.05	0.05
62	1961	1961	0.05	0.05	1961	1961	0.05	0.05	1961	1961	0.05	0.05
63	2059	2059	0.05	0.05	2059	2059	0.05	0.05	2059	2059	0.05	0.05
64	2162	2162	0.05	0.05	2162	2162	0.05	0.05	2162	2162	0.05	0.05
65	2270	2270	0.05	0.05	2270	2270	0.05	0.05	2270	2270	0.05	0.05
66	2384	2384	0.05	0.05	2384	2384	0.05	0.05	2384	2384	0.05	0.05
67	2503	2503	0.05	0.05	2503	2503	0.05	0.05	2503	2503	0.05	0.05
68	2628	2628	0.05	0.05	2628	2628	0.05	0.05	2628	2628	0.05	0.05
69	2760	2760	0.05	0.05	2760	2760	0.05	0.05	2760	2760	0.05	0.05

n													
70	0.05	0.05	2898	2898	0.05	0.05	2898	0.05	0.05	2898	2898	0.05	0.05
71	0.05	0.05	3043	3043	0.05	0.05	3043	0.05	0.05	3043	3043	0.05	0.05
72	0.05	0.05	3195	3195	0.05	0.05	3195	0.05	0.05	3195	3195	0.05	0.05
73	0.05	0.05	3355	3355	0.05	0.05	3355	0.05	0.05	3355	3355	0.05	0.05
74	0.05	0.05	3522	3522	0.05	0.05	3522	0.05	0.05	3522	3522	0.05	0.05
75	0.05	0.05	3698	3698	0.05	0.05	3698	0.05	0.05	3698	3698	0.05	0.05
76	0.05	0.05	3883	3883	0.05	0.05	3883	0.05	0.05	3883	3883	0.05	0.05
77	0.05	0.05	4077	4077	0.05	0.05	4077	0.05	0.05	4077	4077	0.05	0.05
78	0.05	0.05	4281	4281	0.05	0.05	4281	0.05	0.05	4281	4281	0.05	0.05
79	0.05	0.05	4495	4495	0.05	0.05	4495	0.05	0.05	4495	4495	0.05	0.05
80	0.05	0.05	4720	4720	0.05	0.05	4720	0.05	0.05	4720	4720	0.05	0.05
81	0.05	0.05	4956	4956	0.05	0.05	4956	0.05	0.05	4956	4956	0.05	0.05
82	0.05	0.05	5204	5204	0.05	0.05	5204	0.05	0.05	5204	5204	0.05	0.05
83	0.05	0.05	5464	5464	0.05	0.05	5464	0.05	0.05	5464	5464	0.05	0.05
84	0.05	0.05	5737	5737	0.05	0.05	5737	0.05	0.05	5737	5737	0.05	0.05
85	0.05	0.05	6024	6024	0.05	0.05	6024	0.05	0.05	6024	6024	0.05	0.05
86	0.05	0.05	6325	6325	0.05	0.05	6325	0.05	0.05	6325	6325	0.05	0.05
87	0.05	0.05	6642	6642	0.05	0.05	6642	0.05	0.05	6642	6642	0.05	0.05
88	0.05	0.05	6974	6974	0.05	0.05	6974	0.05	0.05	6974	6974	0.05	0.05
89	0.05	0.05	7322	7322	0.05	-0.33	7322	0.05	0.05	7322	7322	0.05	0.05
90	0.05	-0.33	7689	7689	0.05	0.65	4900	0.05	-0.33	7689	4900	0.05	-0.33
91	0.05	0.05	8073	8073	0.05	0.05	5222	0.05	0.07	8073	5145	0.05	0.05
92	0.05	0.05	8477	8477	0.05	0.05	5566	0.05	0.07	8477	5402	0.05	0.05
93	0.05	0.05	8901	8900	0.05	0.05	5932	0.05	0.07	8901	5672	0.05	0.05
94	0.05	0.05	9346	9346	0.05	0.05	6323	0.05	0.07	9346	5956	0.05	0.05
95	0.05	0.05	9813	9813	0.05	0.05	6739	0.05	0.07	9813	6254	0.05	0.05
96	0.05	0.05	10303	10303	0.05	0.05	7183	0.05	0.07	10303	6566	0.05	0.05
97	0.05	0.05	10819	10819	0.05	0.05	7656	0.05	0.07	10819	6895	0.05	0.05
98	0.05	0.05	11360	11360	0.05	0.05	8160	0.05	0.07	11360	7240	0.05	0.05
99	0.05	0.05	11928	11927	0.05	0.05	8698	0.05	0.07	11928	7602	0.05	0.05
100	0.05	0.05	12524	12524	0.05	0.05	9271	0.05	0.07	12524	7982	0.05	0.05
101	0.05	0.05	13150	13150	0.05	0.05	9882	0.05	0.07	13150	8381	0.05	0.05
102	0.05	0.05	13808	13808	0.05	0.05	10533	0.05	0.07	13808	8800	0.05	0.05
103	0.05	0.05	14498	14498	0.05	0.05	11227	0.05	0.07	14498	9240	0.05	0.05
104	0.05	0.05	15223	15223	0.05	0.05	11967	0.05	0.07	15223	9702	0.05	0.05
105	0.05	0.05	15984	15984	0.05	0.05	12756	0.05	0.07	15984	10187	0.05	0.05
106	0.05	0.05	16783	16783	0.05	0.05	13597	0.05	0.07	16783	10696	0.05	0.05

107	17622	17622	0.05	0.05	17622	14494	0.05	0.07	17622	11231	0.05	0.05
108	18504	18503	0.05	0.05	18504	15448	0.05	0.07	18504	11792	0.05	0.05
109	19429	19429	0.05	0.05	19429	16466	0.05	0.07	19429	12382	0.05	0.05
110	20400	20400	0.05	0.05	20400	17551	0.05	0.07	20400	13001	0.05	0.05
111	21420	21420	0.05	0.05	21420	18707	0.05	0.07	21420	13651	0.05	0.05
112	22491	22491	0.05	0.05	22491	19940	0.05	0.07	22491	14334	0.05	0.05
113	23616	23616	0.05	0.05	23616	21254	0.05	0.07	23616	15050	0.05	0.05
114	24797	24796	0.05	0.05	24797	22654	0.05	0.07	24797	15803	0.05	0.05
115	26036	26036	0.05	0.05	26036	24147	0.05	0.07	26036	16593	0.05	0.05
116	27338	27338	0.05	0.05	27338	25739	0.05	0.07	27338	17423	0.05	0.05
117	28705	28705	0.05	0.05	28705	27436	0.05	0.07	28705	18294	0.05	0.05
118	30140	30140	0.05	0.05	30140	29245	0.05	0.07	30140	19209	0.05	0.05
119	31647	31647	0.05	0.05	31647	31174	0.05	0.07	31647	20169	0.05	0.05
120	33230	33230	0.05	0.05	33230	33230	0.05	0.07	33230	21178	0.05	0.05
corr	1.00		0.03		0.99		0.05		0.99		0.04	

INDEX

CPSIA information can be obtained at www.ICGtesting.com
Printed in the USA
BVOW03*0203171013

333889BV00004B/87/P